Beer in the Evening

Beer in the Evening

Edited by Anne Thorniley

FRIDAY
BOOKS

First published in Great Britain in 2006 by Friday Books
An imprint of The Friday Project Limited
83 Victoria Street, London SW1H OH
www.thefridayproject.co.uk
www.fridaybooks.co.uk

British Library Cataloguing in Publication Data.
A catalogue record for this book is available from the
British Library.
10 – 1-905548-05-2
13 – 978-1-905548-05-7

Designed and produced by Staziker Jones
www.stazikerjones.co.uk

The Publisher's policy is to use paper manufactured
from sustainable forests.

Contents

Introduction

Before you go in a pub for the first time, it's difficult to know what to expect. Sometimes you can try to tell from the outside what type of place it is – locals' pub, sports pub, student bar, upmarket wine or cocktail place – but that's not much use. The only real way to know what a pub is really like – what the atmosphere and people and staff are like, when's best to go and when's best to avoid – is to go inside and have a drink. Regularly. Become a regular.

But what if you're new to the area? Considering a move there? Visiting London, or just a different part of London to your normal haunts? How then do you know where to go?

You ask a regular. And that's where we come in. On beerintheevening.com, we have for years given people the opportunity to talk about the pubs that are important to them. We've brought together their opinions in a compendium of comments about London's pubs and bars, written by the people who know best: the drinkers. This isn't a guide to every pub in London or even the best pubs in London. It's a guide to the pubs that people talk about the most, the ones that they really care about.

Finding a pub

We've divided London into a few different sections. They're roughly based around postcodes, but not exactly. Some areas end up in two sections because they cross the borders we've chosen. Trust us, it'll all make sense after a few more beers. Also, if you're after a specific pub or location, you can look in the index at the back of the book.

Central (West)
Belgravia, Bloomsbury, Clerkenwell, Covent Garden, Embankment, Fitzrovia, Holborn, King's Cross, Leicester Square, Mayfair, Oxford Circus, Pall Mall, Pimlico, Russell Square, Soho, Strand, Temple, Trafalgar Square, Westminster

Central (East)
Aldgate, Bank, Barbican, Bishopsgate, Blackfriars, Borough, Cannon Street, Clerkenwell, Fenchurch Street, Fleet Street, Holborn, Leadenhall Market, Liverpool Street, London Bridge, Old Street, Shoreditch, Southwark, Waterloo

South East
Addiscombe, Beckenham, Bexleyheath, Blackheath, Bromley, Camberwell, Chislehurst, Deptford, East Dulwich, Greenwich, Kennington, New Cross, Peckham Rye, Sidcup, South Croydon, Sydenham, Vauxhall

Beer in the Evening

East
Barking, Bethnal Green, Buckhurst Hill, Hackney, Homerton, Leyton, Leytonstone, Limehouse, Mile End, Rotherhithe, Stepney, Stratford, Walthamstow, Wapping, Woodford, Woodford Green

North
Alexandra Park, Angel, Islington, Archway, Barnsbury, Bounds Green, Crouch End, Enfield, Finchley, Finsbury Park, Harringay, Highbury, Highgate, Holloway, Islington, Kingsland, Muswell Hill, Newington Green, Stoke Newington, Tottenham Hale, Wenlock, Wood Green

North West
Baker Street, Belsize Park, Camden, Dartmouth Park, Euston, Golders Green, Hampstead, Harrow, Kentish Town, Kilburn, Primrose Hill, Queens Park, St John's Wood

West
Acton, Bayswater, Chiswick, Ealing, Earl's Court, Hammersmith, Hanwell, Kensington, Maida Vale, Marble Arch, Shepherd's Bush, South Acton, South Kensington, West Ealing

South West
Balham, Brentford, Brixton, Clapham, Collier's Wood, Fulham, Hampton Wick, Isleworth, Kingston upon Thames, New Malden, Parsons Green, Putney, Richmond, St Margarets, Southfields, Stockwell, Teddington, Tooting, Twickenham, Wandsworth, West Brompton, Wimbledon

Central (West)

The Angel

Soho
61 St Giles High Street, London WC2H 8LE
☎ 020 7240 2876

Character, charm and cheap beer; what more can you want? How about a bizarre one-table back room with the allure of a David Lynch movie? Great pub that I never fail to visit each time I'm in London. Quality.
✎ *Trapdoor, December 2005*

Super little pub to pop into during a weekday afternoon, when the affected 'suits' are not in attendance – but even they are worth a smile! As usual, Sam Smith's great beers/prices.
✎ *mikem, August 2005*

Brilliant little pub for those who like it old school, yet fills up with all types of characters, young and old. Has two entrances for the split areas of the pub, so be sure to try both if you're meeting people there for the first time. There's also a large hidden table on the way to the toilets, via that strange cold garagey bit. Good selection of beers. Haven't tried the food but the menu did read of nothing that fancy. Definitely worth a visit.
✎ *Ruby, April 2005*

Nice pub tucked away from prying eyes behind Centre Point. Space is at a premium inside but it's cheap and cheerful in terms of both drink prices and decor. A real old-fashioned boozer that gets its atmosphere mostly from conversation rather than gimmicky entertainment. Being a Sam Smith's pub it serves very little other than Sam Smith's beer, so those looking for more familiar brand names will be disappointed – but they shouldn't be, as the lager is very nice indeed, as are the ales.

✎ *Mr.Monkfish, November 2004*

The Argyll Arms

Oxford Circus
18 Argyll Street, London W1F 7TP
☎ 020 7734 6117

Fantastic-looking pub – faux traditional or real traditional – not sure. A real interesting place to drink. Did have some difficulty getting my order across but that's nothing new these days. A pleasant place to meet friends but one you probably wouldn't linger in.

✎ *Madcap, January 2006*

This place is an oasis. Slap bang in the middle of town, it's ideal for that pint you need after a gruelling Tube journey into town. Plenty of fruities. Nice dark corridor to hang around in and quietly shake.

✎ *tanderson7, March 2005*

Not a bad pub, but when the Palladium turns out it is crazy. Ideal for a train home from Oxford Circus Tube.

✎ *billy124, March 2005*

Manages to be surprisingly good despite being smack bang in the middle of the hell on earth that is Oxford Circus. The interior is interesting (lots of old-fashioned mirrors, corridors, etc.) and the staff are friendly and efficient (they need to be, given how busy this place gets). London Pride is pretty well kept, if slightly unmemorable. I can't remember what the prices were but it certainly didn't stand out as being overly expensive. If you have the profound misfortune to find yourself in the vicinity, then the Argyll is well worth popping into to console yourself.

✎ *Mr Lash, January 2005*

Bradleys

Fitzrovia
42 Hanway Street, London W1T 1UP
☎ 020 7636 0359

Tiny and dark. Lovely place. Great jukebox. Wild Turkey usually available.

✎ *gussetmonkey, December 2005*

Dropped in for a quick couple of pints on the way to a gig at the Astoria nearby and was sorely tempted to give the gig a miss and carry on drinking the night away here. A lovely hidden treasure of a pub just off Oxford Street on the road that loops round to join Tottenham Court Road. Decor was homely and old-fashioned but with a charmingly lived-in feel. Jukebox was excellent and played the kind of stuff that you wouldn't normally hear in a pub. Bar staff were friendly and efficient. Sadly, most of the beers were off when I was there due to the high demands that bank-holiday-weekend drinkers had put upon the place, but the draught San Miguel was delicious. Not overly pricey for a pub in such a prime location either. Well worthy of visiting again and again.

✎ *Mr.Monkfish, May 2005*

You love pubs with atmosphere. You love pubs with good beer. You love Bradleys.

✎ *E1_Norton, May 2004*

Genuinely, one of the best five drinking dens in London. Lovely manager – Mark – and fantastic beer. Make the bloody effort and find it.

✎ *JohnWallace, February 2004*

This, for me, is the best bar in London. Hidden away behind the seething crowds of Oxford Street, it offers a much-needed antidote to the trend for converted bingo-hall sports bars. Bradleys is absolutely tiny and you need to get there early to grab a table in the basement. The jukebox is one of the best in London, the beer is beyond comparison and the atmosphere is everything you would ever want in a bar. If it has one downside, it's the amount of braying, Armani-clad morons who seem to have adopted it in recent months, but they quickly learn to stop banging on about their sales margins and just sit back and enjoy the place as much as the rest of us. Top notch.

✎ *Slipperduke, February 2004*

The Calthorpe Arms

Holborn
252 Gray's Inn Road, London WC1X 8JR
☎ 020 7278 4732

Average interior but well above average Young's. Had a couple of Specials, which were very tasty and not at all winey. Then went on to the normal Best or whatever it is, which was also good. No hangover the next day whatsoever. Very good beer here. Plus, yes they do that mad chocolate beer in bottles.
✎ *danrkelly, January 2006*

Good range of Young's beers in bottles. Seems to be a friendly chilled local. Worth a squirt if you are in the area.
✎ *Stonch, December 2005*

Usually head in here post five-a-side down the road with a couple of lads. Pleasing beers and lagers abound. Usually not too packed and seats outside for when the sun is shining. Top locals' boozer. An unpretentious joy.
✎ *misterpercy, June 2005*

Beer's very good, food's passable – a fine old boozer, with fine old regular clientele to match.
✎ *Claret_and_blue, December 2004*

The Chandos

Trafalgar Square
29 St Martin's Lane, London WC2N 4ER
☎ 020 7836 1401

Went here last weekend to meet a few friends before heading to a mate's birthday celebrations at Covent Garden. Went to another Sam Smith's pub, the Cock Inn, just off Oxford Street about a year ago and had always thought of it as one of the most welcoming London pubs I'd ever been to. I can now add the Chandos to that list. Although fairly empty (it was two in the afternoon), the staff made every effort to make you feel welcome and were constantly moving around keeping the place tidy. I know for a fact that I did a strange double take when the barman told me that two pints of bitter would be £3.40! It was amazing to finally be drinking at a London pub where you hand over a tenner and get over a fiver back in change. The bare-boards look of the place was comfortably inviting and even the toilets were remarkably well maintained. Will definitely be going back.
✎ *palser, November 2005*

Lovely pub with character. Avoids being a tourist trap despite its prime location. It's a Sam Smith's, so the beer is good but unique to the brewery and the famous and premium brand-name drinks are not served here. Lovely wooden-floored area downstairs with nice booths to secrete yourself in. Upstairs offers a warmer, more comfortable environment with more sofa-style seating than standing room. If the windows are open in summertime it's a good place to watch the world go by. Lovely building all in all, with good beer at a very acceptable price. Bar staff are generally on the ball and friendly too.
✎ *Mr.Monkfish, September 2005*

Had a few in here Sunday afternoon. Staff were friendly, the Old Brewery bitter was good, and me and pals passed a few hours pleasantly while London sweltered. The upstairs bar was plush and not busy at all. Very nice. Yay for Sam Smith.
✎ *MrScott, August 2004*

Dark, Dickensian. A good place to take foreigners who want to see a proper London pub.
✎ *Vindaloo, August 2003*

The Cittie of Yorke

Holborn
22 High Holborn, London WC1V 6BS
☎ 020 7242 7670

If you can shove past the city lads and carve out a niche, it has the most amazing interior, cheap cheerful food and good drink selection.
✎ *maddiekat, January 2006*

An excellent pub with atmosphere, something most pubs in London have forgotten about. Tiny snugs for conversation and a fire that was very welcome on a day that was freezing. I expect this place can be packed with city types on a weekday but it was perfect on a Saturday afternoon. Definitely a pub to be recommended.
✎ *Anonymous, December 2005*

Not your typical pub. Nice lounge bar up front but the back bar is what gives the place its reputation. Snug little booths for conversation. Booths have always been full when I have been there (at the end of the working day). Interesting decor. I think it is a well done pub. Sam Smith's is not my favourite beer but the Old Brewery Bitter was OK at my last visit. Hard to beat Sam Smith's prices.

✎ *jorrocks, October 2005*

I first found out about this pub leafing through a c. 1970 book entitled The Cooking of the British Isles. The book used it as an example of a typical London pub and featured a fantastic picture of that famous back bar. I was determined to go and visit this place, if it still existed, but could find no record of anywhere called Henekey's – as it was named at the time the book was printed. I engaged in a fruitless quest over the next couple of years trying to find it. It was only thanks to the Internet that I eventually discovered – to my joy – it did still exist, and was now called the Cittie of Yorke.

The back bar at the Cittie is really just plain fantastic and lives up well to the expectations I'd had from the photograph in the book. It has a well-deserved place in CAMRA's list of historic pub interiors.

✎ *jhawkins, April 2005*

Spent a good evening down in the basement of this place last Friday. The beer was good, food was alright and the staff were kind enough to reserve an area for me and my mates. It's a Sam Smith's pub – you can normally rely on them to be good and the architecture of this one is fantastic. Well worth a visit.

✎ *MrScott, November 2004*

The Coach and Horses

Mayfair
5 Bruton Street, London W1J 6PT
☎ 020 7629 4123

Liked this place, sells Deuchars IPA so gets many points for that. Small trad wooden boozer. Wasn't overly rammed with folk when all the surrounding pubs were so that was a plus. Could probably do with more staff as it was a bit of a tip (dirty glasses piled up on bar, excessive amounts of fag butts, etc. on the floor), but all in all pretty good.
✎ *MrLash, December 2005*

Nice pub. Excellent pint of Pedigree.
✎ *harlequin, February 2005*

Slightly small but very nice.
✎ *mr_lunch, January 2005*

Certainly the best pub for proper ales in the area, and a good place to waste an afternoon while your other half is shopping. Always a good selection of different beers. However, I was in there one Saturday night and they closed at 8 p.m.! How odd is that?
✎ *duncan, December 2003*

The Coal Hole

Strand
91–92 Strand, London WC2R 0DW
☎ 020 7379 9883

Working just round the corner, I have frequently used the Coal Hole to meet friends, spouse and businesspeople and have had no complaints from anyone I have ever taken there ... and there lies the rub. It is a pub that it is difficult to say anything against as it appeals to a wide range of people. Set on the Strand among theatres, etc., it will attract tourists so why do people seem so surprised that this is the case? Reading other reports of how expensive the pub is – rubbish! All Nicholson's pubs appear to have a set price and I have found that it is usually pitched a bit less than the average pub in the surrounding area.

The beers I have had in the Coal Hole have been excellent and the food fine. The decor is interesting and unusual and gives the place its own character. I have never had any problem with the staff or the service in my many visits over the past 18 months and usually manage to grab a seat (try the minstrel gallery if there are none downstairs) or at worst a bit of ledge to place my pint. The only downside that I have experienced is when there has been a convention or meeting in the adjoining Savoy Hotel and everyone piles in at the same time; however, this is not common. It should also be noted that there is a downstairs bar (more of a wine bar) that is worth checking out. They used to have a plasma TV but this has now gone (it's not really a TV sort of pub and it did look a bit out of place anyway).
✎ *RogerB, October 2005*

Fine traditional pub – no complaints. Mr.Monkfish is not wrong – this is the best pub in The Strand.
✎ *JohnBonser, October 2005*

I like the Coal Hole a lot and always have. Nice building with a lot of atmosphere and character. Beer is always good and prices are par for the area. Good mixture of people in there normally and bar service is efficient.

Best place to go for a drink on The Strand. If you can get one of the few seats on the upstairs bit, it's a very pleasant place to settle in for a drink with your nearest and deaest.
✎ *Mr.Monkfish, September 2005*

The Cove

Covent Garden
1 The Piazza, London WC2E 8HB
☎ 020 7836 8336

It should first be pointed out that the Cove is situated in Covent Garden, one of London's premier tourist areas. It should therefore be no surprise to note that the bar is a somewhat cynical touristy recreation of a traditional Cornish smugglers' inn. The bar itself is accessed through a Cornish pasty shop at ground level and is easy to miss (I have been walking past it for 18 months without giving it a second glance and only really found out about it from this website). The bar itself is made out to look like an old boat (maybe it was, but I doubt it) and leads to a further two small drinking bars. The surroundings may be fake but it is comfortable and they have

done a good effort to try and make it feel authentic. Unfortunately there is nothing that can be done to replace the local opera singers and street entertainers with the sound of the sea crashing over the rocks at Lizard Point so an amount of poetic imagination is required. The walls have a nautical theme with portholes, pictures of washed-up ships and old sea captain murals. The seats are a strange combination of comfy chairs, cushioned cubes and sturdy low bar stools. There is an outside veranda overlooking the piazza where there is always a healthy throng of tourists watching the street entertainers. The big plus about this place is the beers. They have five Cornish ales on hand pump (including a wheat beer) and they are reasonably priced considering you are in such a tourist trap. There are two or three standard lagers and Scrumpy Jack cider for the non-real ale buffs. One small gripe is the annoying habit of bar staff handing your change over with a receipt on a plate expecting you to leave a tip. They wouldn't dream of it in Cornwall!
✎ *RogerB, October 2005*

Hidden pub with selection of well-kept, if somewhat cold, Cornish ales from Skinners and St. Austell. Extensive pasty menu available, and balcony from where you can watch the street performers. One of the best pubs I've visited in London. Reasonably priced beer at £2.60 a pint.
✎ *ahscum, May 2005*

They serve HSD – enough said! Get there early in the summer to bag a balcony table and sit back and enjoy the surroundings with good beer and table service from the pasty shop downstairs.
✎ *winkywoo, November 2004*

The Cross Keys

Covent Garden
31 Endell Street, London WC2H 9EB
☎ 020 7836 5185

Nice traditional pub; well worth a visit. Note the Beatles memorabilia.
✎ *JohnBonser, January 2006*

I love this pub. I'm not sure why, but it's one of my favourites in London. Its jumbled and messy and red and it just feels right to be sitting in there on a Saturday afternoon getting slowly drunk. It's got one of the best chip shops in London just down the street from it.
✎ *Jesper, December 2005*

Great pub. Good beer, served well by friendly staff. Interesting decor. Well worth a visit. Puts many other pubs in the area to shame.
✎ *Muffindamule, January 2005*

A nice, usually quiet pub that serves a nice pint. I always try to visit when I am in town. I have never been there when I wasn't amused by some unusual character. The WCs are interesting too.
✎ *saiga, July 2003*

De Hems

Soho
11 Macclesfield Street, London W1D 5BW
☎ 020 7437 2494

Oranjeboom. Yummy! One of the few pubs in central London I'd go out of my way to visit. Does get incredibly packed but it has such a nice atmosphere. Friendly staff and clientele, and excellent range of Dutch beers. And I'll say it again – Oranjeboom. It's just delicious! Late licence too, although I suppose most places will have from tomorrow. Hurrah!

✎ *Cleversaz, November 2005*

Excellent selection of Dutch/Belgian beers – Amstel, Hoegaarden, Leffe dark and blond, etc., and many more. Great to go to a pub with quality available rather than the usual Carling, Fosters, etc. crap.

✎ *lennie384, August 2005*

Lovely boozer. A wonderful reminder of the benefits of living in a cosmopolitan city: a Dutch pub right on the edge of Chinatown. A lovely big old building with plenty of character. Nice wooden floor and a few dark wooden tables and stools, but the majority of punters stand. The beer is excellent. Various Dutch beers on draught, with a wider selection of Dutch and Belgian bottled beer. Bar staff are friendly and do their best to keep the potentially mammoth waiting times down despite the fact that the place is almost permanently busy, especially at weekends. Very nice if you can get in there on a weeknight after the initial post-work crush has filtered out, as you may actually get a seat and easy passage to the bar. At its absolute best when there is an international football tournament involving the Dutch on the telly, as the atmosphere is brilliant. A lovely place.

✎ *Mr.Monkfish, February 2005*

This is a pearl of a boozer in an area not exactly renowned for classy establishments. The lager is excellent and it's rare I get the

chance to say that. Normal West End prices, but that's to be expected. Close to Chinatown – be careful where those post-beer munchies take you!
✎ *Slipperduke, February 2004*

Very central. Very busy. Crowd spills out into the road on balmy summer evenings. Occasionally, Dutch women there.
✎ *Ruby, July 2003*

The Devereux

Temple
20 Devereux Court, off Essex Street, London WC2R 3JJ
☎ 020 7583 4562

A good pub just to pop into. Had a good range of real ales on. Didn't order any food. Service was a bit slow, but when my friend enquired about a beer he was offered a free sample. Thought it excellent that half the downstairs bar is no smoking.
✎ *snowdog2112, January 2006*

Down a characterful dark alley, and full of a good selection of guest ales, which pleased me. Also full of a load of lawyer types, but they're OK I suppose. We didn't try the food but the menu sounded good.
✎ *jaq, February 2005*

They do food until quite late and we popped in to have a sarnie each. Meat-eating mates rate the sausages and other food; the few veggie options are tasty, the chips are good and the beer and staff are all pretty nice. Most of the customers are lawyers and rich kids, but London scruff-bag wizards have found the place and hold meetings in the cool upstairs room most Wednesdays. Beer good – always a couple of real ales on, if you like that sort of thing. What is quite rare for a London pub is that most of the backpacker staff appear to be in a good mood most of the time.

✎ *MrScott, January 2004*

The Edgar Wallace

Temple
40 Essex Street, London WC2R 3JF
☎ 020 7353 3120

☆ RAVE REVIEW

Just about everything a good pub should be – except within walking distance of my house! The bar staff are friendly, knowledge-able and eager to serve you well. This last point really shouldn't be a major differentiator in London pubs, but sadly it is rare enough. The beer – I am a real ale fan – is kept superbly and served at its best. One of the best pints of Deuchars IPA I've ever had. The selection changes regularly – which in some places can be irri-tating as you can't always get what you were looking forward to; however, I have never had a bad pint in this pub and so have come to trust the landlord's choice and judgement.

It is a great shame that they don't have twice the space, but if you have to share a crowded pub with a load of overpaid suits (mostly lawyers in this case) it would be with this lot. Invariably polite and good-natured.

Oh yes, and if you get hungry (and if you are, what are you doing in a pub?) they do really nice snacks and full meals right into the evening.
✎ *Phil Wilson, February 2006*

Cheeky little pubby pub we dropped into before going to a gig at King's College students' union. Good range of beer and nice atmosphere. They do 'English tapas', which we didn't try but looks funny, like 'mini-fry-up' and 'mini-ploughman's'.
✎ *MrScott, November 2005*

An excellent pub. Went there for a few lunchtime drinks. The good range of well-kept real ales made it hard to leave. Nice interior, friendly staff. Looking forward to returning for an evening session.
✎ *duncan, September 2005*

Fitzroy Tavern

Fitzrovia
16 Charlotte Street, London W1T 2NA
☎ 020 7580 3714

Top boozer, good beer and cheap compared with the other pubs in the area.
✎ *fatshirt, November 2005*

Quality beer served at a quality pub. Nice and cosy. Interesting range of beers and lagers, which is typical of a Sam Smith's pub. Nice not to see Foster's, Stella and London Pride for once. Well worth seeking out.
✎ *snowdog2112, November 2004*

Another fab Sam Smith's boozer with bitter and ales under £2 a pint. Bloody marvellous! Great to stand out on the broad street and watch the world go by day or night. Put it this way: I dislike the West End but this is a pleasant oasis.

✎ *danrkelly, May 2004*

The French House

Soho
49 Dean Street, London W1D 5BE
☎ 020 7437 2799

Definitely pretentious but it is a great place and I think everyone should go at least once to see whether they like it.

✎ *Stonch, December 2005*

Lots of people will hate this place. Thank God – there's little enough room for us as it is. It's a good place to be thin. Personally I don't like the John Smith's beer so I stick to the pastis here – they have the excellent HB as well as the usual Ricard. Not to mention the cider – though I don't know whether they're still going to be serving Gavin's Christmas Pudding Vodka, which used to be such a seasonal treat. Best approach to the French is to get pissed quickly and regard the whole thing as a kind of site-specific performance art experience. One of a kind.

✎ *flat3, October 2005*

Tiny, smoky, crowded. They only serve halves. Full of luvvies, journalists, aspirant poets ... brilliant. Ah yes, one of Soho's legendary drinking dens. Where so many new novels have been spoken about but never written; where pretty young wannabe actresses fall in love with inflated, drink-sodden directors. Have been a regular for ten years and still get served by some of the same professional bar staff. Great pub for the booze or the conversation ... vive la French House!

✎ *Tiser, September 2005*

Try the cider from Normandy – really good ... but it sneaks up on you!

✎ *Regis, August 2005*

Comedy Francophile boozer. Check out the clientele smoking Gitanes while drinking Ricard. No joke, I'm serious. If they had a jukebox they'd only have Edith Piaf on it. Like something out of 'Allo, 'Allo!. Priceless.

✎ *ganger, March 2005*

Gordon's Wine Bar

Embankment
47 Villiers Street, London WC2N 6NE
☎ 020 7930 1408

Fantastic. Though maybe not strictly for this site as not sure they do beer. But who cares? The wine is good value for central London (starts at £12 a bottle), and very nice at that. Supposedly they've served it since the fourteenth century so know their stuff. Most of the vaulted cellar has yet to see an electric light, so candles on each table give it a real atmosphere. Nice food as well. Definitely one not to miss.

✎ *OldRogue, January 2006*

Beer in the Evening

I was taken here on a first date and had the best time. The guy's friend said it was a bad idea to take me there but I can honestly say I have never been to such a unique place. I was very impressed. It has such a good atmosphere and great wines. Have been there so many times since then; it's becoming a real local for me and my friends. Definitely worth a visit for any lover of wine and a mystery.

✎ *lucy_k, December 2005*

I tried to educate my lager-drinking friends with a visit to this place. Tried and failed. They downed their bottles in seconds and wanted to move on to a 'proper pub'. Philistines! It's a great place and they missed a treat.

✎ *conniwot, August 2005*

Yesterday, an afternoon glass turned into six hours in the place. The atmosphere is thick; the staff are charismatic and friendly, and certainly not wine snobs. The food isn't cheap, but I would pay much more for this gem.

Although it is always busy, a table always becomes free sooner or later if you hover for a while. It is very private, excellent for clandestine affairs, sobbing on your partner's shoulder, heated debate and whispered plots. And for always finding space for one more stool around a table.

✎ *vinrouge, March 2005*

Amazing place. Handy for Waterloo/South Bank. Knowing this place makes you feel like a London geezer rather than a tourist.

✎ *Vindaloo, August 2003*

The Grenadier

Belgravia
18 Wilton Row, London SW1X 7NR
☎ 020 7235 3074

A well-hidden pub – come equipped with map, compass and preferably a GPS receiver. Probably a good thing it's elusive though, as it's a bit too popular with organised tours already – on the plus side the ale is usually very well kept and the Bloody Marys are truly excellent.
✎ *tim_eyles, January 2006*

Delightful little pub, very well hidden down what appears to be a private mews but full of charm and English tradition. Oh, and did I mention the toffs? Fully expected given its location, and calls for much entertainment, naturally! Well worth a visit if you can find it.
✎ *Cleversaz, December 2005*

I love this pub. Have been here many times and – although it can get very crowded – I have always found it difficult to leave when it is time to go. The food is superb, the ale fine, the staff more than efficient. Go there – you may even see the Grenadier's ghost!
✎ *Mr.Raffles, July 2005*

The Harp

Covent Garden
47 Chandos Place, London WC2 4HS
☎ 020 7836 0291

Beer in the Evening

The Harp (formerly the Welsh Harp) is a fairly small pub that can easily be overlooked due to the proximity of at least four other pubs/bars within 30 yards. This is probably one of the most homely and civilised pubs in the area, with friendly staff and welcoming groups of locals. The pub is long, narrow and full of character. Very much a traditional-style pub, with bare floor, large mirrors, several portraits, brass chandeliers, lamps and stained-glass windows at the front (note the harp depicted in the door). Along one side is a ledge with built-in tables at the rear. On top of the bar frame are several jugs and urns just asking to be shot at like a fairground stall. Entertainment is minimal, with just a basic TV in the corner. There is also a no-smoking room upstairs. The real icing on the cake is the beer: three regular ales (Harveys, Black Sheep and Landlord) complemented by two ever-changing guest ales (a selection of the pump clip-ons can be viewed above the bar). The sausages were very popular, although I did not try one. Definitely one of the best pubs in the area for the serious drinker.
✎ RogerB, January 2006

Excellent. Long narrow pub just north of the Strand and Charing Cross Station. A friendly atmosphere combined with absolutely superb beer makes this a must. Visited last night and had a pint of Black Sheep Bitter which was 100 per cent on form. O'Hagan's sausages are available at the bar and must be tried. Staff very friendly and welcoming. Locals and other customers warm and accommodating. Overall, this is a quality pub, serving quality beer for the quality customer. Recommended. 10/10!
✎ ladnewton, December 2005

Great little pub with excellent staff and a good range of beers. A nice relaxed atmosphere and, as someone else says, customers are not rudely booted out at 11.15 p.m., as in so many Covent Garden pubs. A traditional pub in a central area that boasts very few of them. More power to its (beer-pulling) elbow.

✎ *TJR, February 2004*

The John Snow

Soho
39 Broadwick Street, London W1F 9QP
☎ 020 7437 1344

I have always liked this little place for a quick half of the weisse on an afternoon out and about.

✎ *Stonch, January 2006*

Typical Sam Smith's pub. Close proximity of magazine publishing companies means that Friday nights it's full of young graduates in their first jobs looking for a cheap pint. So lots of kiddies shouting loudly and trying to impress each other. Which can be fun if you're (a) one of them or (b) looking for someone to laugh at. Downstairs area manages to feel cramped even when it's empty, but upstairs is a bit more spacious.

✎ *flat3, November 2005*

A jukebox would be perfect, as long as the Sugababes were banned. Lovely wee pub this. Found it accidentally halfway through a massive sorrow-drowning pub crawl the day John Peel popped his clogs, and it's become an excellent place to start a 'Soho research session'. And that oatmeal stout in bottles that Sam Smith's pubs do – I'm having some of that: marvellous stuff.

✎ *cid, April 2005*

Having background music decided by the bar staff is a Very Bad Thing, as you finish up listening to the Sugababes. Personally, I would rather have no background music; better still, install a jukebox.
✎ *TheGP, February 2005*

Charming little pub. A tad small, but with the usual Sam Smith's drinks, such as Hefe wheat beer and the Old Bloke in the Box. D-Pils for psychos too.
✎ *Ruby, December 2003*

The Kings Arms

Clerkenwell

11a Northington Street, London WC1N 2JF
☎ 020 7405 9107

☆ RAVE REVIEW

The Kings Arms is a traditional London pub. You walk in and immediately feel that things have not changed for a long time – even the regulars. Just look at the floor, which has had a lot of ale spilled over it in the past 200 years. Everybody is friendly – you can easily get in to a conversation or just be on your own if you want. It is also a good sign when you see that women are happy to come in on their own for a drink and not feel bothered. There are usually three real ales on. Greene King IPA, Timothy Taylor Landlord and Adnams Broadside are all served in impeccable condition by the ballsy Aussie landlady. There are two pool tables, a dartboard and table football upstairs, as well as Sky Sports in both rooms. Great Thai and English food is served all day – well worth a try! The pub is open Monday to Friday but is available for private parties free of charge at the weekends, so what are you waiting for? Well worth a visit. Cheers!

✎ *Simon, February 2006*

Nice pleasant traditional side-street pub, just off Gray's Inn Road. Worth visiting, but a bit difficult to find. Has real ales and is CAMRA-friendly. Try the Adnams Broadside if it's on.

✎ *JohnBonser, December 2005*

Go there often. Great traditional London pub. Beer is always well kept and atmosphere is really bubbly, helped by a great Aussie bar-maid. Well worth a visit.

✎ *Anonymous, October 2005*

A great vibe in this pub. The food looked good too. But, best of all, Triv on the games machine!

✎ *dawnage, June 2005*

The Knights Templar

Chancery Lane
95 Chancery Lane, London WC2A 1DT
☎ 020 7831 2660

This is the best Wetherspoon's pub. Lots of nice legal secretaries!

✎ *Linkman, February 2006*

Impressive decor to say the least. Couldn't believe it was a Wetherspoon's when I walked in. Had to go back outside to check I was in the right place. With Wetherspoon's you expect to sacrifice

some class in favour of getting value for money, but there's not a bit of that here. Here you don't get the usual Wetherspoon's crowd (drunks and youngsters who are only there because it's cheap). The grub is the usual Wetherspoon's fare, but looking in the kitchen (you can actually see into this one) it looks clean and encourages you to order something from the menu. There is a wide range of beers and from my experience the guv'nor runs a decent cellar. I note also that most of the others who have reviewed this pub have praised the toilets, and I would not argue with them on that. I have not been in the Ladies (I'm a bloke) but am reliably informed that it is worth visiting the pub just to see them. The Gents are certainly among the best I have visited. All in all I have to say that this is a very nice pub that is worth a visit if you are in the area and looking for good value, a nice clientele and pleasant surroundings. It's not a million miles away from Covent Garden and theatre land either.
✎ *SSSS, January 2006*

A huge space, like a lot of Wetherspoon pubs, but we found a more intimate seat in the rooms up the back. Good-value real ales. I agree the toilets were impressive.
✎ *jaq, February 2005*

The Lamb

Bloomsbury
94 Lamb's Conduit Street, London WC1N 3LZ
☎ 020 7405 0713

Never quite managed to go here without spending the entire afternoon. The food is exactly what I expected of a pub about ten years ago. Not sure if that's a good thing or not. It is a real pub, though

– bizarrely inefficient central bar area, awkward tables, etc. Sounds bad but is in fact good. Good ales on tap and I can't normally be arsed with ale, so there you go.

✎ *gingerweasel, October 2005*

Cracking homemade food! Proper old-school boozer. One of those pubs that I hope never changes.

Problem is that it's in a new-media gastro revamp area but I have a feeling that this is a place that will stay untouched.

✎ *stoner, September 2005*

Been coming to the Lamb on and off for ten years. Being a South London boy, the Young's and the wide range of other beers is always welcome.

Small, intimate place with a good bunch of punters of varying types, and the staff are always friendly. Most of my friends who have visited like the place, and some are real converts. Always give it a look-in when I am in this part of town.

✎ *rebelde, May 2005*

A wonderful place. Great Young's beer – the St George was on top form recently. There is an atmosphere here that has not changed in the 25 years of my occasional visits.

One of the great London pubs to hide away in: sample the beers and consider the history.

✎ *mally, April 2005*

The Lamb and Flag

Covent Garden
33 Rose Street, London WC2E 9EB
☎ 020 7497 9504

Can be tourist-central at times, but a nice enough pub. When tourists conjure up an image of a pub it looks like this one.
✎ *jorrocks, October 2005*

Splendid pub – I have only ever been in three times (including last Saturday) and have never had any problems with the beer or the service. In fact, the standard of the Young's Ordinary would put many of the pubs much nearer the brewery to shame. Also had Ridley's, Marston's and Courage Best on. Still feels like a proper pub, even though it is on the tourist trail. Probably the best pub in this part of the West End.
✎ *JohnBonser, March 2005*

Plenty of history ... and that can mean plenty of tourists on a Friday night. Given its location, you can expect a full house.
✎ *Mr.Matt, February 2005*

A real pleasure to find a proper pub not mucked about with. Ales tried were excellent.
✎ *canastajim, February 2005*

This pub has a really good vibe – a proper pub as it should be.
✎ *TheGP, August 2004*

The Lord John Russell

Russell Square
91 Marchmont Street, London WC1N 1AL
☎ 020 7388 0500

My second visit to the Russell, and this time I've remembered to leave a comment. I don't know the pubs around this area at all, but this one is a nice mix of locals, workers from the local institutions and randoms like myself and Tom. Good pint of Bombardier plus hot pasties and sausage rolls for £1.50. Nice idea. You can lock your bike up on the railings opposite and keep and eye on them through the big picture windows too.
✎ *danrkelly, November 2005*

A natural, old-fashioned and well-run little boozer in Russell Square – now there's a sentence that's not easy to write without a sense of slight disbelief. Seriously though, the Russell has just about everything you'd want in a pub – a very wide booze selection (that runs from strawberry bitter to Kronie Blanc), friendly staff, good clientele and a nice atmosphere that is both welcoming and relaxing. There has been some debate in the comments on the size of the place and just to be a really irritating little sod I'm going to sit myself straight in the middle of the debate. I certainly wouldn't describe it as large or small, though I'd also hesitate to call it a medium size (yeah, it takes me until dawn to decide what I want for my evening meal). In the end I'd go for it being between small and medium, but whatever your personal perspective on this tedious debate it doesn't stop it being a cracking 9/10.
✎ *pgazz, April 2005*

The Maple Leaf

Covent Garden

41 Maiden Lane, London WC2E 7LJ

☎ 020 7240 2843

The food is surprisingly good, if a bit expensive. Staff are very friendly. They only have one cask bitter, but it's a good one – Courage's Best. Extremely difficult to find a table in the evening and impossible if there's any hockey on the TV.

✎ *skorch, October 2005*

Great Canadian pub. Best in the winter when it's cold outside, watching ice hockey on the screens and supping on a cold Molson's draught.

✎ *ganger, March 2005*

OK, you might think that I'm slightly biased due to my English/Canadian dual nationality, which was always likely to draw me to this pub, but I genuinely think it is one of the, if not the outright, best pubs in the West End. A lovely friendly bar populated by natives of London, Canada and beyond that serves good Canadian beers, including Molson Canadian, Molson Dry (both on draught as well as in bottles), Moosehead and Sleeman (no Kokanee or Rickard's, which is a shame) and shows the hockey. The food is nice and reasonably priced. Canadiana in the form of hockey memorabilia and a Mountie uniform adorns the walls, and the back of the pub is decorated so as to resemble a log cabin, all of which may sound tacky but actually works really well. Bar staff are friendly and efficient. Prices are a little steep, but where else are you going to get a pint of Canadian in London? Good for a

relatively quiet drink and a bite to eat on midweek days, but also good for a more lively night out at weekends.
✎ *Mr.Monkfish, January 2005*

McGlynns

King's Cross
1–5 Whidborne Street, London WC1H 8ET
☎ 020 7916 9816

If unfortunate enough to be stranded in King's Cross, this is the place to flee to and take refuge.
✎ *redrocket, October 2005*

I enjoyed my visit here. It is a slightly unusual place, but all the better because of this. The beer was good, even though I am not a great fan of Courage Best.

There is a nice welcome and a good selection of 'real' people (if you understand my meaning). Good to see that the Gents is handy for the bar and the ladies have to trek down the stairs – makes a change!
✎ *mally, April 2005*

Well what can one say about McGlynns? It's got to be the best pub in King's Cross, if not in London. Gerry and his team are the best. Jessy is a fantastic cook and the portions are great too. We hate going out of the Square Mile as we get withdrawal symptoms from our fantastic local.
✎ *davetherave, March 2005*

I visited this pub while on vacation in London from the USA during the beginning of November. This is the best pub I encountered while visiting London. The food was served in a separate room in the back and it was excellent and plentiful. There is a good selection of beer. The staff were attentive and courteous. There was one girl from the Ukraine and one from Poland, and they were hard workers. The customers were friendly. I will return to this pub.

✎ *Winstonunderwood, December 2004*

The Museum Tavern

Bloomsbury
49 Great Russell Street, London WC1B 3BA
☎ 020 7242 8987

Arrived early-ish evening to find fairly busy, with mix of locals and some tourists. Also a combo of both having food – a good sign! Service efficient (for which very pleasantly surprised), with a good range (six) of ales on draught. Add to this a combo of other drinks, lagers and impressive for main tourist area. As a group, we worked our way though all of the beers fairly quickly, with all being in good condition. Also, as the evening went on we were easily able to get a table. Look forward to returning again.

✎ *zakman, January 2006*

Pleasant enough. Very American, although I enjoyed the conversation I had with an elderly Floridian couple with whom I got chatting in there last Friday night. I'd recommend this pub for people who want to be close to the bright lights for a late supper, but have no time for noisy, crowded places.

✎ *dawnage, June 2005*

Very impressive! Great beers on cask. Lovely interior: lots of dark wood and there is room to breathe.

✎ *beerbum63, April 2004*

The Nags Head

Covent Garden
10 James Street, London WC2E 8BT
☎ 020 7836 4678

A deceptively large and spacious corner pub barely 30 yards from Covent Garden market. The Nags Head is perhaps a bit more touristy than some of the other pubs in the area. That is not to say it's not worth a visit – you just need to dodge the rucksacks. The pub is very appealing, with many interesting traditional features: stained-glass windows, bar frame, etched mirrors, alcoves, dim lighting. The decorative tiled floor around the bar immediately draws the attention. The pub is owned by McMullen's Brewery, so it does offer a change of scenery from the usual ales, although it was a bit pricey compared with other pubs in the area (McMullen's Best was £2.80 compared with Young's Best at £2.35 in the White Lion opposite). Plenty of seating – I managed to get a stool even on a Friday lunchtime, although beware of the stools towards the rear of the pub – they are barely 12 inches off the ground and make you feel like a kid at the dinner table.

✎ *RogerB, January 2006*

A bit of a mixed bag, this one. On the one hand this is a nice enough old-fashioned London watering hole, with a reasonable selection of beers, friendly and efficient staff, and a great location. On the other hand, it seems to be somewhat lacklustre, and the atmosphere and value-for-money aspects are not all that they could be. Inexplicably much more popular than it deserves to be. Not that it's bad or anything, but just not quite worthy of being packed all the time and raved about in some quarters, especially given that there are superior pubs within a short walk of here. One plus point, though, is the sight of the local street performers popping in for a pint after their show while still made up as robots, statues, etc. Call me old-fashioned, but no matter how long I continue to live in this wonderful city, things like that always make me chuckle and raise my eyebrows.

✎ *Mr.Monkfish, May 2005*

After visiting many pubs in the area over a four-year period, this is a good find. I like the draught beer and the lively friendly atmosphere and good service. The food (although not cheap, but it is Covent Garden!) is good and highly recommended. I will return :-)

✎ *Anonymous, January 2004*

The Nags Head

Belgravia
53 Kinnerton Street, London SW1X 8ED
☎ 020 7235 1135

Brilliant historic place, this. Tiny but unbelievably quaint. If you walk in here and get a seat (of which there are about 25 in total), then you are sorted. Popped in for an exploratory one last night but have already got it pencilled in for an all-day session some time before Christmas. Tudor beams, roaring fire and quality/simple food prepared in front of you at the bar. Geezer ordered gammon sandwiches last night and a massive joint appeared out of nowhere and was despatched with aplomb by cleaver behind the bar. Like I say: quality place. But get here early if you want to get a seat. I for one shall be banging on the door at 11 a.m. on my next visit. It'll probably be easier to park the horse and carriage at that time as well.

✎ *kmcs, November 2005*

Fantastic, idiosyncratic boozer. A real hidden gem in this otherwise snooty part of London, and one that I can highly recommend visiting. Excellent well-kept beer.

✎ *MarcDickson, June 2005*

If anyone knows of a more perfect pub in London than this one, please let me know. It seems unlikely.

✎ *Hockers, September 2004*

I went in for a quick pint but couldn't bring myself to leave. Excellent boozer with lots of locals.

✎ *Dr_J, November 2003*

The Nell Gwynne

Covent Garden
2 Bull Inn Court, London WC2R 0NP
☎ 020 7240 5579

Beer in the Evening

Absolutely brilliant. The best pub in the West End by miles. The trip to the toilets can be tricky after a few pints though!
✎ *SusanC, November 2005*

One of the smallest and hardest-to-spot pubs in London, sandwiched between two theatres down an alley between the Strand and Maiden Lane. The weathered sign at the Strand end hardly advertises the pub. But for a small plaque on the wall and a humorously written blackboard, there is no indication that there is a pub within the locality and yet it is barely ten yards from the Strand. If approaching from the Strand end, notice the wonderful old tiling on the walls before the alley opens up by the pub. A sign on the pub wall gives a brief history of Nell Gwynne and tells of the murder of an actor outside one of the nearby theatres. The pub is said to be haunted (aren't they all?).

The pub itself is one small room, slightly terraced to take into account the hill down which the alleyway runs. The first thing you notice is that it's dim, very dim, with heavy curtains, dark wooden panelling and wall coverings. The walls are adorned with vintage prints and paintings, some barely visible in the half light. Although small, the pub is well laid out and makes the most of its limited space, even managing to fit in an unobtrusive dartboard. There are two well-positioned TVs, usually showing Sky Sports. I picked a bad time to try the beers: they had just had a delivery and all four hand pumps were out of action, but there was the usual selection of lagers, Strongbow, John Smith's, etc., at typical prices for the area. At least I know they seem to take care of their beers, allowing them to settle before serving. The staff were friendly and welcoming. An excellent, if secretive, pub that is well worth checking out.
✎ *RogerB, October 2005*

Another great night in the Gwynne, or I should say out in the alleyway. Good beer as usual, and when it got too cold and we had to move inside, what a jukebox for an old rock head!
✎ *Gann, October 2005*

Fantastic boozer, this one.

The perfect lunchtime venue, and good for the football as well. It also features those mythical London bar staff who actually want to chat to the punters.
✎ *Hoppo, August 2004*

The One Tun

Goodge Street
58–60 Goodge Street, London W1T 4LZ
☎ 020 7209 4105

A lovely place, and it always was. Young's bitters up to the normal high standard, and even Strongbow is cold and lively. Management and staff have always seemed to change regularly but are always efficient and polite.
✎ *Martinl, September 2005*

Great little pub. Good beer, friendly staff, and often quiet.

A nice place to while away the hours with a good book and a few pints. Never tried the food though.
✎ *jcraf, June 2005*

This is a little gem of a pub, with a magnificent selection of fine ales, cold lagers and European barmaids. I don't know about you, but that ticks a lot of boxes in my book.
✎ *Slipperduke, April 2005*

Jolly nice pub. I agree – the best in the area. Has a dartboard, great beer, some great tunes, friendly staff and landlord. The front opens out when the weather is nice, so you can watch the world go by.
✎ *stuartwigby, April 2004*

This, geekily, is the first pub I've been to on a beerintheevening.com recommendation and it is bloody marvellous. Serves Young's Export lager – why does it taste of fruit? Brass poles and wood panelling abound, as does a lively atmosphere amidst good music, which is heard but never deafening – and a blast from the past, convincing me to buy the 24 Hour Party People soundtrack. Mentioned this site to the barman. Now surely that's worth a pint, mate?
✎ *Ruby, July 2003*

The Pakenham Arms

Clerkenwell
1 Pakenham Street, London WC1X 0LA
☎ 020 7837 6933

Great pub – the lads behind the bar are always briefed on what they are selling. A big working-class contingent (posties in particular) makes up the bulk of the clientele, though there are no stares at the stranger here – they are used to people coming to sample the good, constantly changing range of real ales. Except on Saturday and Sunday, it is open late (and has been for some years), which is great. I have always enjoyed my visits here.

✎ *Stonch, December 2005*

If you like your pubs to be pubs and the beer to be good, this is the place to go. Non-pretentious. It's a pub. Pure and simple. I love this place. Three screens for sport. Cheap drinks and, I hear, good food. Friendly staff. Watched Sunderland get promoted in this pub. Fantastic!

✎ *thebigman, September 2005*

Great for an after-closing pint – late-licence pub catering for the Mount Pleasant posties. Fairly ordinary inside, but good if you've missed your last train. Two big-screen TVs as well.

✎ *M_Evans, September 2005*

This is a super pub. Crisp beer, clean lines and tasty food, and everything is very reasonably priced. The locals are friendly and the bar staff (landlord Michael and manager Gary) are all very welcoming. It has a 'normal' late licence – as in, you don't have to pay to get in there – so it's a jewel in the Norf London crown.

✎ *TheIrishC, May 2005*

The Pillars of Hercules

Soho
7 Greek Street, London W1D 4DJ
☎ 020 7437 1179

I have been coming here for the best part of 20 years and don't think I have ever managed to get a seat in this typical one-room

Beer in the Evening

Soho pub. Originally built in 1733, the present pub dates from around 1910 and retains several features from this time. There is a good range of beers at reasonable prices and served by efficient staff – you rarely have to wait, no matter how busy they are. Food is somewhat limited, but you wouldn't come here to eat anyway. The initial seated area inside the door leads to a bit of a bottleneck adjacent to the bar. Beyond is a further small seated area. The stairs to the toilets are reminiscent of a cliff face. Despite the obvious cramped conditions, the atmosphere is very friendly and welcoming. It attracts a mixed bag of customers and is often populated by music fans, the Astoria, Mean Fiddler and Borderline all being within a stone's throw. Such is its popularity, there are usually twice as many people drinking outside on the pavement than there are crammed inside the pub. Definitely worth a visit.

✎ *RogerB, October 2005*

Often referred to as the 'Gateway to Soho', for reasons that are obvious if you approach from Foyles. If you can catch it at a quieter moment (or, better still, when the famous DJ is in residence), this is a surprisingly decent pub given its location and owners.

Beers are usually excellent, and they normally have a good range. Internal layout means it can feel cramped at times, but it is the best in the area.

✎ *flat3, October 2005*

Still a nice little pub in the heart of Soho – though big emphasis on the word 'little'. Don't go here if you're fat! Also, good selection of real ales – well, would have been but out of the four, two were 'off'.

✎ *Darren_in_the_City, March 2004*

The Porcupine

Leicester Square

48 Charing Cross Road, London WC2H 0BS

☎ 020 7379 9855

A great place to meet – it's next door to Leicester Square Tube. The staff have every right to be unpleasant (very busy at times), but they're surprisingly friendly. Some decent ales on too. Also good for people watching if you're alone.

✎ *Terry_W, November 2005*

Quite a small pub for the area, so can get a little cramped. Just opposite Leicester Square station, so a good meeting place to kick off a pub crawl.

✎ *lennie384, February 2005*

Crowded downstairs, but there were tables free upstairs so we sat there and enjoyed the view up Charing Cross Road. A good traditional pub.

✎ *jaq, February 2005*

The Porterhouse

Covent Garden

21–22 Maiden Lane, London WC2E 7NA

☎ 020 7379 7917

The beer list is simply amazing, with some amusingly candid descriptions of certain piss-poor well-known brands found in other pubs. Expensive? Not the cheapest, but then you can easily spend £3 on a bog-standard Stella anywhere else round there, plus figure some of these beers aren't on the usual distributors' lists. Cruzcampo may be 50p a litre in Spain, but then we're not in Spain (sadly). Blame Gordon Brown! It's good to see somewhere modern and vibrant promoting genuinely interesting and unusual beer.

✎ *OldRogue, January 2006*

Boisterous Irish bar on three levels. The beers start at about £2.80. Pub absolutely heaving at 8 p.m. last night. The atmosphere is lively, and even the bouncers were friendly when I visited. Try the TSB and Oyster Stout. Interesting furniture and lighting.

✎ *ladnewton, December 2005*

This place is excellent – so much to choose from on the beer menu! The food is pretty good too. Best drink I've tried there is the Porterhouse Red. Heaven in a pint. OK, prices are bit steep, but it's Covent Garden, not Hull. At least you get something unique for your cash. It does get crowded, so best to go in mid-Sunday afternoon to enjoy the place properly. One slightly sore point – watch their quizzer if you take more than a quid out of it: it sets ridiculous levels of attainment for the next time. Win your money and go!

✎ *Quinno, August 2005*

A great pub. Shame about the location. Loads of fantastic beers – even a decent beer from Australia! Loads of little nooks and crannies to hide in. Unfortunately, it's right by Covent Garden, so as a result gets too full. Also, the bar staff could do with some kind of 'punter awareness' programme. Don't stand in the wrong place: you'll be waiting for a loooonnnng time!

✎ *mattmbaker, March 2004*

Strange place. Dark, cavernous and crowded. Chairs and tables become a much-sought-after commodity and once gained are rarely given up all night. Good choice of beers from what I can remember, which ain't much.

✎ *Ruby, July 2003*

The Prince of Wales

Pimlico
91 Wilton Road, London SW1V 1DW
☎ 020 7233 8898

Truly excellent old-style boozer in a very unpromising area for that sort of pub. Good, if unexceptional, selection of ales (Greene King IPA, London Pride, Adnam's The Bitter and Old Speckled Hen), but really good ambience and surroundings.

✎ *Joe_Cundy, January 2006*

A place you're happy to spend a few hours in – something rare in the public-house desert that is Victoria. Staff are friendly and efficient and the beer is decently kept.

Worth a look, but don't all come at once because it's too small for all of us.

✎ *davidb, April 2005*

The only pub in the area without television: they pride themselves on this. So not the place to go if you want to watch football, but an OK place to have a drink.

✎ *beeronaut, June 2004*

The Princess Louise

Holborn
208–209 High Holborn, London WC1V 7BW
☎ 020 7405 8816

A beacon of style, good service and value quality ale. Sam Smith's in top condition at £1.70 a pint. The question is: if Sam Smith's can do this in a central area at these prices and still make a living, then what mugs are we for frequenting the £2.50+ a pint merchants? Support those who keep the price of good beer down!
✎ *mally, November 2005*

Excellent architectural features. Sam Smith's beer. Pleasant staff. Too dark. 7/10.
✎ *Real_Al, November 2005*

Great staff. Great beer. Beautiful inside. A 'must see' when you are in the area.
✎ *beerbum63, October 2004*

Go for the loo. Stay for the pint.
✎ *Dr_J, October 2003*

The Red Lion

Pall Mall
23 Crown Passage, London SW1Y 6PP
☎ 020 7930 4141

Splendid pub – well worth a visit. Highly recommended for its traditional atmosphere and warm welcome.
✎ *JohnBonser, March 2005*

Went there with some friends on a Wednesday night in January and ended up staying to closing time. Because of the small size of the pub, we were standing for the first hour or so. Excellent Adnams, reasonable Bass. Small moan – no proper crisps, only Pringles at £1 for a tiddly little pot.

What no one has mentioned so far is that this pub has one of the widest range of whiskies I have ever seen outside of a Scottish hotel behind the bar.

Definitely an unspoilt traditional English boozer that deserves to be visited at least once (and to have a preservation order slapped on it to keep it just the way it is).

And while we're going on about the Gents: mind your head if you are over six foot tall!
✎ *MarcDickson, January 2005*

Brought the wife here after following the guard up to St James's. A true gem, friendly patrons and staff, and a nice Adnams for a cold and weary guest. Not on the tourist track, but right where you want to be.
✎ *Wild_John, December 2003*

It is a very pretty pub. Small and crowded at midday. Very friendly staff.
✎ *saiga, September 2003*

The Red Lion

Westminster

48 Parliament Street, London SW1A 2NH

☎ 020 7930 5826

Traditional pub – enjoy it whenever I am in the area. I have been fortunate to be there during off-hours so have been able to enjoy the pub rather than fight the crowds. Fits Westminster well.

✎ *jorrocks, October 2005*

Dropped by in the evening and saw a good mix for patrons: government types in ties, tourists in comfort clothing, and various friends and relations. All seemed to be having a good time. Good ale selection and at a fair price for London. The pub fits into its surroundings well.

✎ *Mr.Matt, July 2005*

Rammed full of tourists drinking coffee when I was there on a Saturday lunchtime.

✎ *marty_mac, March 2004*

The Royal George

Charing Cross Road

Goslett Yard, 133 Charing Cross Road, London WC2H 0EA

☎ 020 7734 8837

Found this pub a great place to go during the daytime/early evening. It is not too busy. Prices are what you expect for West End pubs. Note that they stop food at 3 p.m. and then start again at 5 p.m., which left me hungry. Haven't ventured there in the night yet, but am planning to soon. Staff are friendly and I had no wait to get served. They play good music as well.

✎ *stripe, December 2005*

This is a great little pub – a real find in the middle of central London. I just happened upon it one day when looking for a loo after shopping. The 'oddness' that others have mentioned is its real bonus. It's a bit arty and different, which is a real breath of fresh air after the hundreds of bland boring chain pubs that central London is plagued with.

If you want a nice plain ordinary bar, then go to All Bar One. If you want the staff to smarm all over you with a fake smile on their faces, then go to TGI Fridays or some such place. If you want an interesting decent pub to have a quiet pint (or a good night out with a lively atmosphere – depending on when you go), then I'd definitely recommend this little gem.

✎ *Curly_Helen, July 2005*

The Salisbury

Strand
90 St Martin's Lane, London WC2N 4AP
☎ 020 7836 5863

Encouraged by recent postings, I went to the Salisbury on a Thursday night and am pleased to report that standards are being maintained. The beers (we had Tribute and Bombardier) were excellent, the door staff courteous – bag searches were as friendly as it's possible to make them – and we were served within a minute of standing at the bar (not bad for a crowded pub). Add to that the amazing etched mirrors, unobtrusive background music and efficient air-con and it added up to a welcome alternative to other West End offerings.

✎ *MarkW, August 2005*

Part of a Friday-afternoon pub crawl after lunch at Vertigo 42. Have been in there before but the decor never fails to impress. Place was pretty empty (having avoided the lunchtime rush) but it was a pleasure to be served by such happy and attentive staff – everyone coming in was greeted with a smile. Pub cosy and with pleasant background noise of staff laughing and satisfied customers chatting away. The fact that you can't hear cars and buses flying by outside also makes this place seem a world away from the hectic bustle and crowds of London in general and Leicester Square/Covent Garden in particular. Fully recommended.

✎ *palser, April 2005*

Historic late Victorian pub with etched-glass windows and big decoration over the main entrance. Used to be several more rooms than the three there are now and has a staircase that goes straight up from the bar like a chimney – which is not too popular with the fire brigade, so the upper floors are apparently empty. Odd lighting, with a mixture of red and amber shades being reflected in the mirrors along the walls, which takes a bit of getting used to. Good (although expensive) ales, including a guest (St. Austell when I was there).

✎ *lout_from_the_lane, February 2005*

Gets rammed in here Friday/Saturday night, but still definitely worth a look. A proper London pub. Of all the central West End pubs, this is one of the most atmospheric. Yes, it is a bit touristy, but this is the West End – what do you expect?! Worth checking out just for the decor – there are not many pubs left this well preserved from the Victorian period (first converted to a pub 1898).

A favourite with the theatre crowd – you might spot the odd famous face having a pre-/after-show beverage in here.

Best position in the pub is the front nook with the tiny bar. Ideal for a little crowd of, say, ten odd to plot up in. But be advised: to get seats in there, you will have to turn up early doors.
✎ *krylon76, January 2005*

The Seven Stars

Chancery Lane
53–54 Carey Street, London WC2A 2JB
☎ 020 7242 8521

Nice snug traditional pub much frequented by the legal profession. Don't use the upstairs loo if you're a bit the worse for wear – descent perilous!
✎ *JohnBonser, January 2006*

Great pub if there is room or it's warm outside. Good beer well kept.
✎ *writtleman, November 2005*

Nice snug pub with loads of atmosphere. Had a nice pint of Adnams The Bitter here. The stairs to the upstairs toilet are a challenge!
✎ *jorrocks, October 2005*

The Ship

Soho
116 Wardour Street, London W1F 0TT
☎ 020 7437 8446

I recently revisited this place after an absence of several years. Until the mid-1980s, it was handy as a meeting place for the old Marquee Club that was situated a few doors down. Along with the proximity of all the major film companies, you could always count on a bit of celebrity spotting. Today it still retains its classic rock angle and can best be described as a more civilised version of the Intrepid Fox further down the road, where the music is more suited to extreme tastes in metal. At the Ship expect to hear the likes of Guns N' Roses, Kinks and Black Sabbath from the well-stocked CD collection behind the bar. One important rule – no dancing (there are signs up just in case you fancied a quick head-bang, and the local council will jump on the pub like a ton of bricks if such deplorable behaviour is witnessed). Instead, watch the sad old rockers of yesteryear (like me) tapping fingers on the bar while sampling the good range of Fuller's beers like the good mature real-ale tasters that we have all become (go on – admit it!). The pub itself is three or four rooms knocked through, but despite being a reasonable size does not offer much in the way of seating. There are a few tables towards the rear but, unless you are early enough to grab a stool at the bar or along the ledge running down the side of the pub, standing is the order of the day when busy. The carpet, windows and general decor are perhaps looking a bit tired but give the place a lived-in, homely sort of feel, with plenty of old pictures. If the walls could speak, there would be a few good stories about this place – Keith Moon was apparently once a regular. Although those days have disappeared (like the Marquee), it is still worth a visit, as it does offer something alternative to the so often bland, plastic, clubby bars that are springing up all over with alarming frequency.

✎ *RogerB, January 2006*

Trad thin and long London boozer. Well-kept cellar.
✎ *W980501, June 2005*

Excellent bar staff. Friendly atmosphere. Usually filled to the brim on Friday nights. Very eclectic music being played. One of the cooler pubs in central London.
✎ *Wayne_Jordan, June 2004*

The Ship and Shovell

Strand
1–3 Craven Passage, London WC2N 5PH
☎ 020 7839 1311

Very busy place but in an ideal location for lots of West End attractions without the prats. I really like it and the staff are friendly and efficient. Very pleasant on a Saturday lunchtime.
✎ *Nailed, December 2005*

A wonderful treat – wander through the arches and up to the pub. Liked the Fursty Ferret on offer.

Busy but not overwhelmingly so, particularly considering the masses thundering up and down Villiers Street. Well worth a visit.
✎ *jorrocks, October 2005*

Very good pub for real ale – it's a Badger pub and very un-London in many regards.
✎ *BigPete, September 2005*

A decent London pub split into two on either side of a narrow alley. Quite unusual, good beer and food, and a cosy place to be in the winter. Best near Charing Cross for a post-work drink.
✎ *vinrouge, March 2005*

A bit difficult to find at first, but well worth the effort. Beer is always on form and the staff friendly and polite. The smaller bar is open as well at busier times.
✎ *TonyAle, December 2004*

The Ship Tavern

Holborn
12 Gate Street, London WC2A 3HP
☎ 020 7405 1992

Traditional pub. Used to have clandestine Catholic Masses upstairs, back in the day. Was a bit disappointed in my Theakston Best Bitter during my last visit. It was a rather dull pint.

Can't comment on the cellar as do not frequent the place often enough to judge.

✎ *jorrocks, October 2005*

Delightful on a Saturday afternoon. Pop in and you may, if lucky, meet characters who seem like the 'two Johns' off Bremner Bird and Fortune – John Fortune and John Bird – in light-hearted banter with the Rumpoles of the Bailey of this world. The Ship is now open on Saturdays but still closed on Sundays.

✎ *mikem, October 2005*

Went there last night to watch the cricket on my way to Smiths. Easy to get served, friendly staff, and a good view of the television (which is refreshingly not enormous, thus keeping out the All Bar None crowds). Only stayed there for a short while but will go back if I am in the area.

✎ *mr_lunch, September 2005*

St. Stephens Tavern

Westminster
10 Bridge Street, London SW1A 2JR
☎ 020 7925 2286

High Victorian-style pub. A recent refurbishment has paid off nicely. Grade 2 listed pub. Excellent Badger Ales on tap.

Well worth a visit if you're in the area.

✎ *jorrocks, October 2005*

Very neat and tidy pub, with nice selection of Badger Ales. Looks enormous when approaching from Westminster Tube, but only two tiny rooms (unless there's an upstairs). I liked it.
✎ *Boothers, September 2005*

Beautifully restored pub and a great location – which add up to make it a really busy place at peak times. The beer's decent and so's the food. At least half a dozen tourists came in to take photos of the place when I spent an evening here a few weeks ago. Recommended.
✎ *davidb, April 2005*

Good pub recently reopened in High Victorian style. Three or four real ales. Sandwiches made with fresh bread – not soggy. Good on a spring Sunday for watching tourists go by.
✎ *beeronaut, June 2004*

The Star Tavern

Belgravia
6 Belgrave Mews West, London SW1X 8HT
☎ 020 7235 3019

Excellent pub, which I have been visiting for the past 25 years and it still looks like the same pub, thank goodness. It has survived the recent change of landlord unscathed. The Fuller's beers taste very good, as of course they should, but all too often don't. Considering the wealthy neighbourhood, the prices aren't that outrageous.
✎ *southdown12jack, December 2005*

Fine pub. Good choice of decent beers (as you would expect in a Fuller's pub). Comfortable interior – excellent place to while away a few hours over several jars.
✎ *MarcDickson, June 2005*

Went down here on Friday night. Not too easy to find, but what a lovely pub. Friendly, cosy, buzzy – everything you could want from a good local.
✎ *libero, October 2004*

Found this pub while looking for somewhere for a quick beer before a meeting in Belgrave Square. So impressed I dragged everyone back afterwards and we spent the entire evening there. Really good pub, well-kept beers and good food. Looking forward to the next meeting.
✎ *Millay, September 2003*

The Toucan

Soho
19 Carlisle Street, off Soho Square, London W1V 5RJ
☎ 020 7437 4123

One of my favourite pubs. It's tiny and smoky but has charm. A more genuine Irish pub than the chains that pop up all over the place.
✎ *nido, June 2005*

Tiny tiny bar. Not bad though, although if raining could cause a problem.
✎ *TheGP, August 2004*

Best Guinness in London. Cracking Chelsea-supporting barman in the evening. Magners on draught. What more could you want? Apart from United winning the league again.
✎ *JohnWallace, February 2004*

Lovely little pub. Ignore upstairs and head straight for downstairs. Really good Guinness, friendly staff and somehow manages to stop short of being patronisingly 'Oirish'.
✎ *Slipperduke, February 2004*

The Yorkshire Grey

Fitzrovia
46 Langham Street, London W1W 7AX
☎ 020 7636 4788

Absolutely lovely. At the back there's a lovely open fire with leather snugs. Barman was really, really friendly, if a bit odd. Sam Smith's Old Brewery Bitter was (a) cask, (b) very nice and (c) £1.70 a pint. Definitely worth several squirts.
✎ *Stonch, February 2006*

The pub time forgot – especially given how close to Oxford Circus it is. If you like collecting pub experiences, go and have a drink and revel in its randomness – it will be a cheap experience if nothing else. Probably at its best in summer, when you can sit outside.
✎ *OCW, December 2005*

I think it was only me and my mates here on Saturday night. There were all the Sam Smith's faves, although they didn't seem to have any of the super-duper new organic ale. Nice floral exterior, trad pub interior. Great for a quiet drink just a few steps away from the madness of Oxford Street.

✎ *MrScott, August 2004*

Central (East)

The Artillery Arms

Old Street
Bunhill Row, London EC1Y 8ND
☎ 020 7253 4683

Have had many after-work drinks in here over the years. Lots of 'suits', but not at all cliquey. Good beers and friendly service.
✎ *timkholman, January 2006*

Wonderful, wonderful little gem of a pub. Great if you work where I do, as you can nip here of a lunchtime or after work and feel you have fully escaped the city. It is situated overlooking a lovely leafy cemetery – resting place of William Blake and Daniel Defoe. Great in summer when you can stand outside in the quiet street.

Does a good range of Fuller's beers (Chiswick, Pride, ESB) plus seasonals and the wonderful 8.5% Golden Pride in bottles in the fridge. Beers are a decent price for the area. Good mix of people – office workers mix with locals nicely. Good craic when it is busy, which it normally is.

The food seems fairly decent too, though at lunchtime it's tough to find somewhere to sit.
✎ *Stonch, December 2005*

Excellent pub – highly recommended. London Pride in fine fettle. Welcoming, friendly and traditional.
✎ *JohnBonser, February 2005*

Pleasant local with central bar and several rooms around it. Well-kept ale. Chiswick good as an opener before the Pride and Winter Warmer. Was in there mid-evening on Friday but it didn't seem overly busy – presumably between the early and late crowds, or did we mingle into them as we had a few?
✎ *lout_from_the_lane, February 2005*

The Banker

Cannon Street
Cousin Lane, London EC4R 3TE
☎ 020 7283 5206

Good place to go for that all-important after-work drink.

Nice location, good selection of beers and a layout that lets you talk to your friends but still carries a lively atmosphere.
✎ *Matthew_of_Ham, December 2005*

The first time I visited the Banker was a couple of years ago. Back then, I thought it was a good pub – decent beer in an excellent (and unique) location. The only flaw was it closed at 8 p.m. I went there again last night with friends and am pleased to report that it stayed open till late, making it an excellent venue to hole up in for the evening. The outside terrace is also blessed with some fearsome heaters.

Goodness knows how much energy they were consuming, but I was quite happily sitting outside in shirtsleeves after 9 p.m. In October.
✎ *MarcDickson, October 2005*

Outside terrace looking towards Southwark Bridge is good. Beer's pretty reasonable – Pride on tap and the like. Worth a look just because it's right under Cannon Street station and part of the inside looks out under the bridge. Dead after 8 p.m. though.
✎ *danrkelly, September 2004*

The Blackfriar

Blackfriars
174 Queen Victoria Street, London EC4V 4EG
☎ 020 7236 5474

This was marvellous! Some nice guest ales, cool decor, odd-looking building. Every pint I've had in here has been top notch. Loved it. Will take foreign visitors.
✎ *mitomighty, November 2005*

This is the exception to the rule. I typically avoid pubs near train stations and Tube stops. This one is a must-see. The marble, alabaster and reliefs of the monks are pretty cool. The Timothy Taylor Landlord is worth going back for alone. Standard Nicholson's menu items.
✎ *jorrocks, October 2005*

I recently made my first visit since the pub went smoke-free. I thought the new policy only enhanced what is already a great pub experience.

It did not seem to detract from business as the place was packed as usual with the after-work crowd and this was a Thursday night. I hope other establishments consider a smoke-free alternative.
✎ *Anonymous, March 2005*

A classic pub with well-cared-for real ales. Always had good friendly service, good food and too much really good ale. In the summer it can get arms and legs, with the crowd spilling out on to the pavement. That just adds to the atmosphere. Quite possibly the most architecturally beautiful pub in London. The marble has to be seen to be believed.
✎ *Zaphod, November 2004*

The Counting House

Bank
50 Cornhill, London EC3V 3PD
☎ 020 7283 7123

Wonderful interior. Absolutely heaving – but that is my own problem for going during the Friday evening rush hour. Beer was very good – seasonal range available too.
✎ *mally, May 2005*

Great environment for a beer and good Fuller's served well by friendly staff. Just an oasis in the City that should never be missed.
✎ *writtleman, April 2005*

Superb pub. One of the most interesting interiors of any of the central City pubs. What I love about it is that it has a zone for whatever drinking head you have on. You've got your propping-up-the-very-attractive-bar option, having a chinwag with the lads/colleagues. You've got your very posh and cosy-looking chairs round the edges of the main ground-floor level, ideal for watching the punters come and go and looking businesslike if that's what you like. You've got your rooms out the back, which have the vibe of an old drawing room/drinking club, very atmospheric and a good place to sit and have a smoke and a chinwag.

Then, of course, you have the upstairs, which is superb to take a little group of drinkers to and plot up in, or perhaps a lady for that intimate cosy chat. The best of it up there is that you can look down on the punters below and just people-watch, and there are lots of little nooks in which to merrily consume your drink of choice.

Love it! And a fairly mixed crowd.

✎ *krylon76, January 2005*

Pretty spectacular interior with a great domed roof, loads of seating downstairs, up on the balcony, and in a couple of decent-sized rooms at the back. Really well-kept Fuller's beer (which one would hope to expect from a Fuller's flagship in this location).

Menu is standard Ale&Pie fare but none the worse for that. Long bar and plenty of staff ensure quick service even when it's busy – only criticism is that it can be a bit 'blokey' but still one of the best pubs in the city.

✎ *MrLash, November 2004*

Dirty Dick's

Bishopsgate
202 Bishopsgate, London EC2M 4NR
☎ 020 7283 5888

Well beat me with a jambock! Stopped in for a beer just before lunchtime. The downstairs bar was very quiet, cricket on TV, some light music filling the room and the Saffa barman having the fundamentals of the 24-hour clock explained to him! It was OK for a quick stop-off I guess, and I feel that I must have arrived too early as the place was unremarkable ... except for the fact that I paid three pounds for a pint of lager for the first (and hopefully the last) time in my life.
✎ *harlequin, October 2005*

Good, authentic old-fashioned City boozer. Gets pretty rammed downstairs but there's always a table to be had on the first floor – and by the time this shuts (early), the crowd downstairs has generally thinned. Usual range of Young's beers, kept well. Food is good, if on the pricey side (and it's not really the sort of place you would come to on expenses).

This and the Shooting Star (round the corner) are a lifesaver at this end of the City.
✎ *MrLash, November 2004*

Great pub and in my opinion serves the best bitter in the Liverpool Street area. One of the few around here to have ambience, but the early closing of the upstairs bar is annoying.
✎ *wpjh, October 2004*

Excellent beer. I was drinking the wonderful Christmas Pudding Ale last Thursday as they still have some left over. The food upstairs is great fodder – especially the Barnsley chop. I will continue to drink in this pub for as long as I live. Love it.

✎ *PieFace, April 2004*

Good range of Young's beers, both draught and bottles. Good atmosphere and one of the better City pubs.

✎ *Millay, February 2004*

The Dovetail

Clerkenwell

9 Jerusalem Passage, London EC1V 4JP

☎ 020 7490 7321

Wonderful place. Totally unique in London. Gets very busy and a little bit too packed sometimes. When there aren't many people around they put on some nice chilled jazz in the background. It's perfect, though depends on when you go.

The food is very good and good value. The service is unsmiling but technically good.

The beers – amazing. I went for a weekend in Bruges recently and the best bars there weren't really much better than this in terms of beer selection.

You have to try it, but not on a Friday night.

✎ *Stonch, December 2005*

I've been here about once a week for three years. I love Belgian beer – lots of practice in Belgium ;-)

I've never found the staff or service to be anything but friendly. They're even urbane when asking people to leave – on the few occasions I've seen it done.

They carry a good, and slowly changing, range of over 100 Belgian beers, at reasonable prices (for Belgian beer in the UK), and any member of staff who's been there longer than a week knows the range well and how to serve it.

Their food is always excellent, for carnivores or vegetarians, and good value.

The decor is eclectic (which is very trad Belgian) – although I'm not sure the latest bout of tiling was an improvement. I usually hate music in bars, but not here.
✎ *JollyGreenGiant, July 2005*

The Duke of York

Clerkenwell
156 Clerkenwell Road, London EC1R 5DU
☎ 020 7837 8548

Excellent pub away from the 'suits' who usually fill the pubs in the area. Staff have lots of character and the Thai food is great and a bargain. Excellent place to while away a weekend afternoon as well.
✎ *mrfalafel, January 2006*

Busy pub with long tables – ideal for a sociable drink. Pool table.
Big, bright. And reasonable beer.
✎ *Anonymous, July 2005*

East India Arms

Fenchurch Street
67 Fenchurch Street, London EC3M 4BR
☎ 020 7265 5121

Had a few lunchtime beers at the East India recently. It was busy,
but the service was still very good, and the beer was in good shape.
A 'proper' pub.
✎ *rockstar, December 2005*

A no-nonsense traditional stand-up boozer. Great!
✎ *BinBagBob, February 2005*

Slightly shabby old-style City boozer for standing up and drinking in.
I wouldn't bother asking for a glass of wine for the lady, as they'd
probably think you were taking the mickey.

Tasty Eastern European barmaids; tasty London Pride. Fine by me!
✎ *MrLash, December 2004*

Proper pub for men to drink decent bitter in. The last time a bird
went in here was 1989.
✎ *PieFace, September 2004*

The Foundry

Shoreditch

84–86, Great Eastern Street, London EC2A 3JL

☎ 020 7739 6900

Certainly the most unique pub I've had the pleasure to while away an evening in, in London. It is more of a squat that sells beer than a pub. The staff are open-minded and friendly and downstairs is an artistic space, where anyone who 'thinks they can do better' is encouraged to do so.

This place makes me think how Shoreditch probably was in the short period when it really was cutting-edge and before the trust-fund babies and hangers-on caught wind of it.
✎ *mikez, December 2005*

The perfect antidote to the seeping poison of the area's shiny style bars, the Foundry is a true one-off.

Situated in a former bank and filled with found furniture, often unsettling artworks and seemingly random items from the street, it looks and feels a bit like a squat but is none the worse for that. Interesting and varied crowd. A place of rare integrity.
✎ *Hal, June 2005*

Interior is like a bank where the shopfitters have bailed out halfway through a revamp. That's because it is! They serve Pitfield ale brewed locally. Worth a look. Great 'intellograf' in the toilets – just made that word up. Irritating isn't it?
✎ *danrkelly, May 2004*

The George

London Bridge

77 Borough High Street, London SE1 1NH

☎ 020 7407 2056

Nice pleasant place to visit in clement weather so you can sit outside, people-watch and admire the frontage. Beer was average, well-served and promptly so. Lunch served through hole-in-the-wall arrangement at end of the pub. All that can be said of that is that it was 'nourishing and substantial'. Worth a look in.

✎ *almost_an_old_git, November 2005*

I like this pub. The staff are friendly and competent without being anything special, but I think it's the aura of the place that is so attractive (well, that and the beer). I'm not sure that it is the oldest pub in London though. The Prospect of Whitby and Ye Olde Cheshire Cheese are both regularly put forward as the holders of that title. Would definitely come back to this tucked-away pub. Well worth a visit.

✎ *womble54321, October 2005*

First visit last night to what I am told is the oldest pub in London (is this true?). Thought it and the pub was alright. Felt sorry for the poor sods who work in the offices in the square who spend all day looking down on the drinkers. Ha ha!

✎ *Darren_in_the_City, July 2005*

A historic pub, tucked away from view. Takes years to get served, but quite enjoyed it nonetheless.

✎ *TheGP, September 2004*

The Green

Clerkenwell

29 Clerkenwell Green, London EC1R 0DU

☎ 020 7490 8010

What a find! The Green bar now also has a separate dining area upstairs, serving a delicious and interesting menu for very reasonable prices. I recently had a fantastic evening meal with hearty soup and melt-in-the-mouth salmon cooked to perfection. Both the restaurant and the bar area have a warm friendly evening atmosphere and the decor is cosy yet elegant. The staff were really helpful and the clientele seemed laidback and friendly. They have a great selection of interesting wines and some unusual draught beers too. Definitely a great cheery place to defeat the winter blues.

✎ *Anonymous, November 2005*

Great beer and good food. City prices but *big* portions of yummy pies and roasts and all sorts of hearty stuff all served up in nicely low-key surroundings with friendly staff. Recommended.

✎ *Gibboski, November 2005*

The Hole In The Wall

Waterloo

5 Mepham Street, London SE1 8SQ

☎ 020 7928 6196

A welcome oasis in a swamp of theme bars and lost tourists. Six ales on tap, though two are from Adnams, and I think Young's

Bitter was on too. Didn't see the alleged Battersea Ale, though. On the whole, this pub is a good meet-up for a couple, before moving to somewhere a bit more youthful. Yes, the constant train noise from above makes this a unique boozin' experience.

✎ *darloexile, December 2005*

A bit of a weird place. Walls are decorated with sick-as-hell cartoons by an artist known as Glen Baxter, and there's a mirror to remind you of the name of the pub. Seems like a lot of people come here for a drink after work.

Very good for beer, with a wide selection of real ales, including the Young's beers and London Pride, all more-than-drinkable beers. A few I've never heard of, which is all the more reason to try them!

If nothing else, stop here for a pint. You won't regret the experience, especially if you're an ale fan.

✎ *Will2, November 2005*

Proper no-frills pub for proper people – it does what it says on the tin. I love it to bits and I suspect you will too. The Adnams Broadside is recommended.

✎ *JohnBonser, October 2005*

Obscured by the vast Waterloo Station, this is indeed a charming find. An old-style boozer with a great atmosphere, two bars and a tiny bog. Not the place to bring your stilettoed girlfriend, however. It's a friendly and sociable place, which belies its slightly forbidding appearance. Think Charles Dickens and you'll get an idea of it's Victorian ambience.

✎ *cider_murray, July 2005*

This truly was a great find. Discovered when tired and hungry with aching feet after the rugby parade and got a warm welcome, a cold beer and a very cheap (especially given the location) filling, traditional English meal. Always worth a stop-off after a day wandering round town when your feet ache so much you don't think you can quite make it to Waterloo without some refreshment. Well hidden and one of the few open-plan pubs with atmosphere. Pop in for a beer before journeying home.

✎ *Cleversaz, February 2005*

The Jerusalem Tavern

Clerkenwell
55 Britton Street, London EC1M 5UQ
☎ 020 7490 4281

This place is getting so packed these days I am tempted to give it a 0/10 just to steer people away. Every time I go these days, they only ever seem to have a best, a golden and a fruit beer on draught – no mild, no cream stout, no honey porter.

This time last year they always had at least two of those on. Slightly annoying when you can't get in the door because groups of office workers exclusively drinking lager are in attendance.

✎ *Stonch, February 2006*

A cool place. Very good beer and friendly waiting/bar staff. The one table loft up the stairs and across from the bar is probably one of the coolest interior pub spots in all of London (a primitive bookend to the Blackfriar's marble/alabaster room).

Wonderful selection of St. Peter's brews ... also for sale in bottles at the bar to take home.
✎ *chipawayboy, January 2006*

I've always gone for the beer and have finally tried the food. Great. Wonderful pub, good food, great staff. One of my favourites, but yes – smoke-filled. 9/10.
✎ *Real_Al, January 2006*

I love this pub. A real-ale drinkers' palace. Serves St. Peter's beer and must be one of the only places that does. Well worth a walk from Farringdon Station. Been there a number of times and the atmosphere is always welcoming.
✎ *TheHorsesMouth, October 2005*

If you want real ale in a pub that is back to basics but nice and cosy, this is the place.

No Foster's, Stella Artois, John Smith's, etc. served here. Well worth seeking out. The only pub I know of where people are standing on the pavement outside drinking in February. Can get smoky if busy.
✎ *snowdog2112, February 2005*

The King's Arms

Southwark
25 Roupell Street, London SE1 8TB
☎ 020 7207 0784

Nice pub. A lot quieter at lunchtimes.

Seventeen years ago the scene of the great Dalek battle
(see *Remembrance Of The Daleks* if you don't believe me!).
✎ *PunkySi, December 2005*

After a smashing summer-evening stroll down the South Bank,
you don't want to spoil it with a numbing chain-pub experience or a
crap pint with the wannabes at the NFT. The King's Arms is well
proper. We loitered around in the evocative Windmill Walk and Roupell
Street just suppin' some ale and cursing the occasional driver who
insisted on using the road (tut!). I had gone off Fuller's London Pride in
recent years, but they serve an excellent pint here. Also available at the
time was Adnams The Bitter, Spitfire and another guest ale I fail to
recall. Before, I used to shy away from the Waterloo area, fearing
chattering tourists and sticky Wetherspoon pubs – but no more. P.S.
Thanks to Elliot for showing us the way.
✎ *danrkelly, July 2005*

A wonderful pub in a brilliant, almost time-warp location (like being
back in the 1960s). Service is fine and the beers OK. One of the
best pubs south of the river.
✎ *andrew1961, January 2004*

The Lamb Tavern

Leadenhall Market
10–12 Leadenhall Market, London EC3V 1LR
☎ Telephone 020 7626 2454

The meeting point for the insurance world. Known to every broker
and underwriter in the City. Young's pub serving excellent ale.

At lunchtimes always surrounded by 'suits' drinking outside. If you are a 'man' and you like to get served quick, go down to the cellar bar, which is always a bit quieter. Two dartboards.

✎ *TheHorsesMouth, October 2005*

Excellent venue for lunching. The Young's is invariably spot on and the beef or pork rolls are first-rate. The only real complaint is the tendency to get over-packed on occasion.

✎ *Moose58, August 2005*

Fantastic Young's pub slap in the middle of the wonderfully atmospheric Leadenhall Market.

✎ *BinBagBob, February 2005*

Great old-style City boozer. Well-kept Young's ales, legendary roast-beef baguettes. Fills up with brokers from Lloyds at lunchtime, but punters spill out into the Victorian covered market so there's never an issue with space. Non-smoking upstairs I believe. Tricky spiral staircase up to the loos after a crafty lunchtime sharpener or three ... If you like All Bar One, etc., please stay away.

✎ *MrLash, October 2004*

The Lord Clyde

Borough
27 Clenham Street, London SE1 1ER
☎ 020 7407 3397

Everything a pub should be. Decent beer, friendly staff, nice atmosphere. Not the biggest of pubs, but there always seems to be somewhere

to sit. The kind of place you can happily while away a wet January afternoon.
✎ *gatecrasher, January 2006*

A good selection of ales, which are invariably in excellent condition. Great atmosphere, particularly on a darts night.
✎ *ChrisF, December 2005*

Yup, great pub. After just one Friday-night visit, it's right up there. Two guys who were playing darts when we got in there disappeared shortly after, only to return later with the gorgeous Keira Knightley in tow. Obviously not in tow like some old water tender or similar.
✎ *danrkelly, November 2005*

I'm getting dead fond of backstreet boozers. This is a find. Locals' pub hidden in Borough. It's like popping back in to the early 1980s' world of pubs. A bit rough but well worth it.
✎ *MrScott, July 2005*

Splendidly traditional unspoilt local. On the CAMRA Regional Inventory for its outstanding architecture, both inside and out. Five draught beers on – Young's Ordinary, Shep's Spitfire, Fuller's London Pride, Greene King IPA and Adnams. Highly recommended.
✎ *JohnBonser, March 2005*

The Market Porter

London Bridge
9 Stoney Street, London SE1 9AA
☎ 020 7407 2495

Cracking good pub. A great mixture of people, from young ladies to old blokes holding the *Good Beer Guide*. One of the best selection of ales I have come across in central London. Staff friendly and helpful. Mouth-watering ales. Will be visiting again soon.

✎ *darloexile, December 2005*

The place was packed when I visited. A ringing endorsement for the pub. Nice location. Well-kept cellar. Spent most of my time standing outdoors with the rest of the herd.

✎ *jorrocks, October 2005*

Wow! This pub is like the Tardis now. Still the same size on the outside but now huge on the inside. Ten (yes T-E-N!) real ales available – making this the only place you need for a pub crawl. Definitely one of the best – if not the best – pubs in the whole of London.

✎ *Darren_in_the_City, July 2005*

Refurb has happened – pub reopened tonight. Now ten guest ales plus Harveys as the regular house bitter. General atmosphere unchanged.

✎ *canastajim, June 2005*

Took one step inside this pub and thought 'I am going to really like this place.' I was right. Great selection of ales and a fantastic atmosphere.

✎ *TonyAle, February 2005*

Real-ale Mecca in London, with an ever-changing range of eight real ales, including Harveys Best Bitter. Service usually good, but can get wedged on the evenings. Currently selling lots of hoppy beers from Archers (Swindon).

✎ *Simonf, June 2003*

The Old Bank of England

Fleet Street

194 Fleet Street, London EC4A 2LT

☎ 020 7430 2255

Nice commercial refit. I usually am not a fan of the bank-turned-pub, but it works here. Can get a bit loud. Worth a look and a pint just to soak it all in. Not a classic pub but works at its own level. Has an outstanding ESB here.

✎ *jorrocks, October 2005*

Love this pub – food is yummy and cider not bad either.

✎ *misty_night, February 2005*

Very grand and ornate interior, although the exterior is shrouded in scaffolding at this time. Friendly staff, crowded with suits, but lots of room for all. Worth a visit.

✎ *MissKitty, December 2004*

The Pride of Spitalfields

Shoreditch

Heneage Street, London E1 5LJ

☎ 020 7247 8933

Brilliant little 1950s time-warp pub – it's cheap and it's a great alternative to all the trendy media-type bars that otherwise populate Brick Lane if you fancy a nice quiet pint pre- or post-ruby.

✎ *baggyjim, November 2005*

Bugger it! Thought this pub was the best-kept secret *ever*. Fantastic pub despite being a bit out of character for the area. Only place for miles that regularly does Crouch Vale beer.

✎ *persist_artist, November 2005*

Top pub. Serves the best pint of beer in the area, and the service and ambience are amazing. Place feels like someone's front room. Popular with both locals and people out for a curry in adjacent Brick Lane. If you fancy a quick pint before or after your Madras, this is the place to go. Great whisky selection too. Counted at least 15 different single malts.

✎ *TheHorsesMouth, October 2005*

One of the last bastions of a community and culture in retreat. A priceless place where the beer was impeccable (Crouch Vale) and the company genuine and friendly.

A perfect haunt to reflect on bygone East End days.

✎ *mally, May 2005*

What an excellent find. A gem. A salt-of-the-earth cliché, etc. Seriously, a very warm trad cockernee pub with no tat or pretensions, and a great mix of people. Even mad old man. Loved it.

✎ *E1_Norton, May 2005*

The Railway Tavern

Liverpool Street
15 Liverpool Street, London EC2M 7NX
☎ 020 7283 3598

This is a great boozer. First-class service even when full, as it is most of the day. Well-kept Greene King ales and a good wine list.
✎ *leggless, November 2005*

A nice big pub that is well worth investigating if you find yourself stuck waiting for a train in the area. Modern decor without trying too hard to be trendy. Flat-screen TVs dotted liberally throughout make it a good place to watch the football. The background music is just that – not set at conversation-killing levels. Not as pricey as some in the area, but still not exactly cheap. The mezzanine level is a great spot for a quiet chat or people-watching and has very comfy sofas; however, negotiating the narrow metal spiral staircase becomes difficult when laden with drinks from the bar downstairs and even more challenging once the drinks have been consumed. The cigar dispenser machines are a nice touch. Has several hand pumps dispensing a wide variety of beers, all called London Pride and all tasting suspiciously like London Pride. Decent variety of lagers and spirits though. It was clean and service was quick and pleasant. Only real down side was the food. I was in there at about 6.30 p.m. and half the menu was unavailable at that point, although they serve food virtually all night.
✎ *Mr.Monkfish, January 2005*

Fantastic busy pub showing all sporting events. A must if you find yourself in the area, and even worth travelling for.
✎ *Emmett, November 2003*

The Royal Oak

Borough
44 Tabard Street, London SE1 4JU
☎ 020 7357 7173

Wonderful pub, relaxed and civilised. Harveys beer is quite possibly the best in Britain – and the Royal Oak sells the full range. Try the Mild or the Old Ale – absolutely delicious and very rare treats in London. Why can't all beer be this good? If you want to stand up necking a bottle of Bud whilst listening to techno, go somewhere else.

✎ *Mr. SOBA, January 2006*

The Royal Oak is a rare example of an unspoilt Victorian boozer, but with the added attraction of top-drawer beers courtesy of Lewes's Harveys Brewery. Tucked away in a not-so-attractive housing estate off Borough High Street, you would not find it unless you are specifically heading for it. The exterior is that of a typical Victorian corner pub with no real discerning features, but once through the front door you enter a classic Victorian lobby resplendent with etched-glass windows. The inside is divided into two rooms by a central bar. The room to the left of the lobby is the smaller 'comfy' bar with interesting photos and prints (note especially the old interior pub photos by the Gents). There is an original fireplace with books on the mantlepiece, more etched windows and a few stools at the bar. To the right of the lobby there is a more open area, with seats and tables by the picture windows and a larger area to congregate at the bar. The beers are all top-notch Harveys bitters. Although they do the usual run of lagers, etc., about 90 per cent of the people in the pub during my visit were all drinking the bitter, which says something about the quality of the beers. The food looked very good, was reasonably priced and was still being served beyond 8 p.m. The pub has no modern thrills, no games machines, no music, no pool tables and no dartboard – just sensible, friendly customers and staff. Many Victorian pubs have lost their shape and character through various refurbishments over the years, but the Royal Oak is the real McCoy. Make an effort to visit.

✎ *RogerB, November 2005*

A true gem. The porter was outstanding. You know it's a great place when you feel as though a short time has passed and then you check the watch and three hours have passed. Truly a great pub.
✎ *Anonymous, March 2005*

In my view, possibly London's finest boozer. The seasonal Harveys ale last night was in fantastic condition and the home-cooked dinners were exceptional. The steak and ale pie is an absolute must. With a huge new estate rising from a giant crater across the road, this part of town will soon be transformed from the back of beyond that it is today, so it is hoped that this little gem never changes. It's a terrific pub.
✎ *SteveinLondonSeptember 2003*

Well worth seeking out. Always a friendly greeting. The appropriate Harveys seasonal beer usually available, and decent food possible at hours most pubs don't want to know.
✎ *canastajim, July 2003*

The Shooting Star

Liverpool Street
125–129 Middlesex Street, London E1 7JF
☎ 020 7929 6818

Decent place with good service and friendly atmosphere. Like lots of City pubs, don't be put off by large crowds at 6-ish ... the tables turn over pretty quickly so if you don't find a seat straight away be prepared to give it 20 minutes or so.
✎ *Anonymous, October 2005*

An excellent lunchtime menu (homemade pies highly recommended) in an easy-to-find location just a stone's throw away from Liverpool Street Station. Good Fuller's beer. Staff a little slow to get to you, but when they eventually do service is quite friendly.

Even though it was a peak lunch-hour rush, I was still able to find a table. Food arrived very promptly, I hope to return very soon.
✎ *CJB, January 2005*

The Still and Star

Aldgate
1 Little Somerset Street, London E1 8AH
☎ 020 7702 2899

Good pub; excellent fast service. Great pub in the summer.
✎ *Anonymous, December 2005*

Great little pub for the beer-drinker. One I visit on a regular basis, especially in the summer, as you can stand outside. Doesn't really have a garden – just a plot next to the bus terminal.

But if you are a City worker looking for a pub in the summer to stand outside, there is nowhere better. Great service, excellent ale. Cheap for area.
✎ *TheHorsesMouth, October 2005*

The Everards Tiger went down a treat.
✎ *carterse9, October 2004*

The Sutton Arms

Barbican

6 Carthusian Street, London EC1M 6EB

☎ 020 7253 0723

First-class pub run by a great landlord who clearly knows precisely what he is doing. Recently started serving Fuller's ESB – couple that with Leffe on tap and a range of Belgian bottles in the fridge and you are on to a winner. Food is good too. Great place.
✎ *Stonch, December 2005*

Went on a Saturday night. I didn't mind that we were the only people in the pub. Perhaps 6 p.m. is too early for some! It got a pleasant crowd, though, and decent beer. It's in a great area too. I suspect a different vibe in the week though.
✎ *mitomighty, November 2005*

This pub is now open on Saturday. Hooray! Can get very smoky and crowded on Thursday/Friday evenings; otherwise to be recommended. Bar food is a bit pricey (sausage + mash = 8 quid), but it's good quality. Good beer. Not full of loud City types.
✎ *jhsp, February 2005*

Had a good meal upstairs with a decent pint. Can't comment on the main bar as on the day we just walked through to the stairs at the back so as to dine.

Are planning an early return (and hopefully more lengthy stay downstairs).
✎ *lout_from_the_lane, December 2004*

The Swan

Bank
77–80 Gracechurch Street, London EC3V 0AS
☎ 020 7283 7712

One for the ale-drinkers. Excellent Fuller's house with two bars. Both very small. In my opinion, probably the best ale in this part of the City. I love it.
✎ *TheHorsesMouth, October 2005*

Magnificent pub for men in suits to drink possibly the best London Pride in the City. Has a bit of a locals' feel to it but so long as you're recognised as 'one of us' (i.e. you're male and in a suit), then there's no hassle. I only checked out the downstairs bar, which is pretty tiny (it would feel crowded with ten people in there), but the decor is authentic flagstones, dark wood, etc., and – correct me if I'm wrong – feels uncontrived as it's been like that since the year dot. I foresee a long friendship with this pub – marvellous.
✎ *MrLash, January 2005*

A small pub, which somehow fits in a cellar somewhere. Good Pride and an escaped Spaniard for a barman.
✎ *gryn, March 2004*

The Three Kings

Clerkenwell
7 Clerkenwell Close, London EC1R 0DY
☎ 020 7253 0483

Beer in the Evening

A unique treasure hidden away in Clerkenwell. They even keep the outside lights dimmed to make it hard to find for first-time visitors. Despite that, it's quite friendly. And it's *the* place to be on a warm summer's evening when you can take your pints outside and sit on the church steps across the street. Quite simply one of the very best pubs in London.

✎ *mrfalafel, January 2006*

Remember that old Eiffel Tower in a snowstorm that Aunt Agnes brought back from Paris when you were a kid? Well give it to the Three Kings. They will find a loving home for it alongside all the other weird, quirky, tacky, unusual and downright eccentric bric-a-brac that can be found lining the shelves and windowsills. A plastic rhino head casts its eye in a watchful gaze over the candlelit bar. A plastic Chinese lion waves gleefully underneath it. Pictures, posters, mirrors and flyers advertising anything and everything fill in any space on the walls that is left. Anything that looks out of place is well suited to this pub. I would not like to be the cleaner who has to dust everything, but I am quite happy to be a customer, sampling any of the three well-kept beers. The rest of the single-room main bar is quite basic, with bare floorboards and plain decor, and it is fair to say that the interior is, in its own way, pleasantly grim. There is an upstairs but I didn't have time to sample it. Full of character and set in a village-type area of London. This is one of the more unusual pubs in London and well worth tracking down.

✎ *RogerB, November 2005*

A joy of a pub – one of the best in London. The downstairs is eccentrically decorated and you can also spill out on to the green. There's also a fantastic upstairs, which hardly anyone seems to know about. So sssshhhhhhhh!

✎ *MrScott, August 2004*

The Wheatsheaf

Borough

6 Stoney Street, London SE1 9AA

☎ 020 7407 7242

What a strange pub it is too. The Market Porter up the road has claimed a lot of the passing suits, all of the tourists and plenty of beardy CAMRA beer-spotters. The Wheatsheaf may actually have all the local market porters and traders drinking in the place.

It's a Young's pub that is mostly a corridor making a U-shape around a bar. The wood panelling and strange hair of the regulars (it is a right regulars' pub) give it a strange feeling that you're looking into the past, which is interesting.

Drank Young's Christmas Ale. It was pretty rich and tasted of currants.

Bit crowded for us.

✎ *MrScott, December 2005*

Loads of character and a (rare sighting these days) dartsboard directly outside the toilets. Expect to see people wandering about with darts in their head! It really has got something unique about it. The layout appears to encourage mingling and chatting to strangers.

Feels like a true freehouse, without all the identikit food chalkboards that blight British pubs. Brilliant.
✎ *TomAngel, June 2005*

What a little gem of a pub! Attractive old building with a saloon and public bar. No pretensions – just friendly atmosphere, good service and superb pint of Young's Special. How a pub should be.
✎ *Tuna, April 2004*

Now a good Young's pub (since 1999/2000?). Was once a much better freehouse (unofficially) owned by Bass Charrington, but the maverick enterprising landlord kept an excellent range of guest beers on. Sadly the pub was always threatened with closure due to the works going on above and around it, so Youngs' purchase of the property was actually something of a reprieve. Starting in this pub, continuing at the Market Porter and finishing at the Royal Oak in Tabard Street makes up an excellent crawl.
✎ *ladnewton, April 2003*

Ye Old Mitre

Holborn
1 Ely Court, off Ely Place, London EC1N 6SJ
☎ 020 7405 4751

Loved this place for a sneaky pint at lunchtimes during work. You have to duck under parts of the place, it is that low in parts. Old wooden beams and a village-like atmosphere – brilliant.
✎ *M_Evans, January 2006*

Brilliant little pub. If you like old pubs, this is the best in the area. Combine this with a visit to the Ye Olde Chesire Cheese and the Seven Stars and you will be in heaven.
✎ *Stonch, January 2006*

My favourite London pub. It really has to be seen to believe just what a tiny space it is squeezed into. The only access is down a tiny alley from either Hatton Garden or Ely Place, and it's a complete gem. Last visited on a Monday afternoon, when it was really quiet; it then filled with office workers, but I know from previous visits that it then becomes quieter and really cosy later in the evening when all the suits have scooted home on the trains. Well worth a visit.

✎ *oxenhillshaw, September 2005*

Oh, and ask for their 'history sheet' to get an excellent rundown of the past 500 years. City pub, so it's closed weekends. Don't be put off by the crowds outside in the alley: there's usually a seat inside. There's two rooms and another level upstairs. You'll get a table, don't worry.

✎ *kodabar, August 2005*

This is a true classic. It's been there since 1546. The cherry tree, which Queen Elizabeth I maypole-danced around, is still there. Cheap, decent, well-hidden. Great selection of guest ales. Heartily recommended to all, except for the fact that I don't want you there spoiling it. You'll never find it anyway. Come off the Tube at Chancery Lane and head south towards 'the Gherkin' and the river. Turn left up Hatton Garden and then cross the road towards the bent lamppost with the bishop's mitre on it. And there you go. Tell Scotty I said 'hello'.

✎ *kodabar, August 2005*

Hidden down an alley in Hatton Garden lives the pub that time forgot. It's still divided up into different sections and looks like it's not been done up since the 1970s. I love a wood-panelled pub that sells pickled eggs.

✎ *MrScott, July 2004*

Ye Olde Cheshire Cheese

Fleet Street
Wine Office Court, London EC4A 2BU
☎ 020 7353 6170

Visited last Saturday. A few tourists in the front bar and a couple of folks snapping pictures here and there ... but it is no surprise that they come ... a truly antique and authentic feel to the place. I'm not sure if there is another pub in London that can take you back (way back) in time the way the Cheese can. Seemed to be a lot of folks eating from a pretty extensive menu. Visit the place and have a bitter, but think of the visit as more of an educational experience than a night out.
✎ *chipawayboy, January 2006*

Sam Smith's pub – so cheap but not to everyone's taste. Incredible interior. It's almost possible to get lost in the warren of different rooms downstairs. Inevitably, due to its location, it never feels like anybody considers it to be their local but it is usually lively enough. Overall, a real gem of a pub.
✎ *gjs34, October 2005*

A great experience, like stepping back in time. There are several bars on several levels, providing a truly traditional service. I went with my father after he had told me of the delights he had experienced after spending a good day's drinking there when he was a 'youth'. I highly recommend the lager and the pub in general. It's a must-visit. Make the effort. Truly great!
✎ *cannon1882, February 2005*

Best pub ever! So much character. You can easily get lost in the maze of catacomb-like rooms if you're not familiar with the place. It's down an alley off Fleet Street. Keep your eyes open for the black-boxed sign next to the King and Keys.

✎ *jaykoivu, April 2004*

South East

The Amersham Arms

New Cross
388 New Cross Road, London SE14 6TY
☎ 020 8692 2047

Thursday nights here are some of the best to be had in SE London. The live impromptu jazz/bluesy stuff is well worth the three quid. The staff are a great laugh – ended up dancing with some last week. Always meet some very interesting characters.
✎ *dwaine, January 2006*

Great pub for watching the famous Glasgow Celtic. Ended up in Lewisham on a Tuesday drinking with a mad Scotsman after going for one pint with a college friend on a Sunday morning.
✎ *keep_it_green, April 2005*

Good proper Irish boozer. Used to have the best Guinness in London although the standards seem to have slipped recently. Definitely worth a look though.

Nice big screen for the football and The Weakest Link and The Simpsons.
✎ *brasco, January 2005*

The front bar is full of hard-core Irish locals, but the back bar (with a big 'Catapult Club' sign above it) does ace musical events. I was walking past on Sunday, saw some blokes playing, had a pint, listened to some free blues and headed home. Nice.
✎ *MrScott, January 2004*

The Anglesey Arms

Bromley
90 Palace Road, Bromley, Kent BR1 3JX
☎ 020 8460 1985

Wholly concur with previous posts. Hidden gem of a boozer and well worth a visit.
✎ *sussexsketch, August 2005*

A smart, well-maintained, friendly Shepherd Neame tavern off the beaten track. Far superior to the more easily sought-after Bricklayers Arms. Staff are welcoming and steak sandwich specials were excellent at £3 a piece. Interesting wall-hangings of Napoleonic history, etc. Beer was of high quality, Shepherd Neame Spitfire, Master Brew and the seasonal Early Bird graced the pumps but slightly stung the pockets at around £2.50 a pint. Sport shown on two medium-sized TV screens but not allowed to take over. All in all, a quality boozer.
✎ *young_camra_collectiv, May 2005*

This is one of the real back-street gems around Bromley North. Until recently, this pub was small, real small. Around November 2004, it was expanded to about double the size, but it has still managed to retain the small backstreet-pub feel.

A Shepherd Neame pub whose beer is always served perfectly and by friendly staff. Always very clean and has also recently expanded the beer gardens (one in the front and one at the rear).

The only downside is that when busy, the pub can become very, very smoky. Although the recent expansion and carbon filters added have helped, it can still be quite dense. If it were not for this, I would have rated the pub 10.

✎ *joeadams, December 2004*

The Ashburnham Arms

Greenwich
25 Ashburnham Grove, London SE10 8UH
☎ 020 8692 2007

A good pub that grows on you. I have it on good authority that the food is all done in house, not from some frozen time-capsule production line. It certainly tastes like the real deal. Good mix of customers, from toffs to your average punter. Well worth a visit.

✎ *jackthelad, February 2006*

I finally found the Ashburnham Arms after a number of misses. I expected your basic back-street boozer – but it ain't. The bar area is light and airy, the Shepherd Neame ales were in good shape, and the food was good and reasonably priced.

I appreciated the stack of newspapers and magazines for when you want to kick back and read. I'm certain this place gets packed with yuppies, but I doubt the regular crowd are high-street types:

you have to really want to find this place, and if you want good ale and good food it's not a bad choice.
✎ *martineaux, November 2005*

Yay for back-street Greenwich pubs.

Nice beer and a nice vibe, but the decor is a little bit B&B-ish.
✎ *MrScott, May 2004*

The Beehive

Vauxhall
51 Durham Street, London SE11 5JA
☎ 020 7582 7608

Spent the evening in there after the Ashes win at the Oval.

Friendly staff and I'll definitely be back there again.
✎ *MikeyBee, September 2005*

With sumptuous decor and good selection of wines, beers and food, this is a very classy pub. Prices are a bit steep, but this ensures that the riffraff stay elsewhere, so you can usually find a seat. Good outside seating area, and the toilets are as lavish as you will find in a pub.
✎ *Chris F, August 2005*

One of the better pubs in the area, and you are usually able to get a seat. Courage Best usually kept better than their Directors.
✎ *Anonymous, April 2005*

The Bishop

East Dulwich
27 Lordship Lane, London SE22 8EW
☎ 020 8693 3994

I love this pub. The staff are lovely and the service is excellent.
The food is good and reasonably priced. Long live the Bishop.
✎ *hooley, September 2005*

Went here last night with a few mates, and it was really nice. The
staff were cool and didn't sneer at us, which we often get at the
Dog. Really friendly. I had the ham and brie sandwich and it was
sooooooo damn good – really tasty. One of my friends had the
burger and said it was very very tasty, and the other two had the
unleavened bread with hummus and said it was excellent.
Good music, good vibe, I love it. Just not enough sugar in the
cheesecake for our liking. Sorry. But I'll definitely come back,
because I love it. Go Bishop!
✎ *elmothelime, May 2005*

Went to this pub for the first time on 25/03/05. It had just
reopened after a major refurb – you could still smell the fresh paint.
It's a very cool bar with a good selection of drinks. Didn't try the
food so can't comment on that. However, I must say that the staff
were excellent. Prompt, friendly and faultless service. The publican
took the time to remember many patrons' names (on a very busy
night), which was a particularly nice touch.
When I'm next in the area, I'll certainly be dropping in.
I recommend you do too.
✎ *wilbur101, March 2005*

The Bricklayers Arms

Bromley
141–143 Masons Hill, Bromley, Kent BR2 9HW
☎ 020 8460 4552

Been in here a few times. Strong lager. Been in there on Saturdays before going to Bromley FC games with a few others. Nice and quiet drink before match days. Went there on a Tuesday night – was quite busy but still enough room to spread out.
✎ *casual66, January 2006*

Been meaning to check out this place for quite a while and was pleased I made the effort after going to a nearby fireworks display. Interior is subtle enough and warm. I do like the central positioning of the bar and the differing levels work well. Staff were friendly and the beers were fabulously kept – the usual high standard for Shepherd Neame. I very much enjoyed the seasonal special, Late Red, and I'm told the Oranjeboom was also good.

Make sure you visit The Bitter End Off Licence next door afterwards – great range of keg-kept ales always changing.
✎ *young_camra_collectiv, November 2005*

The Castle

Camberwell
64 Camberwell Church Street, London SE5 8TR
☎ 020 7277 2601

One of the best bars in Camberwell, although the music seems to be getting increasingly louder, to the point where it is now impossible to hold a conversation after 9 p.m. on a Friday. This is a very nice bar to drink in, especially on a random midweek session.

The food is excellent and is prompt, even when the place is busy. When it is quiet, the bar staff often take your order at the table, which is a good thing as there is a large range of comfy sofas throughout.

Gets busy but seems to be used by most as a post-11 p.m. pub so it is quite easy to get a seat, even around 8–8.30 p.m., or so it appears to me.

✎ *the_sarah_day_fan_club, September 2005*

This place used to be the Snug Bar, which I loved. At first, I was very disappointed when the Snug closed down and the Castle took its place. Where the Snug was cosy and cave-like and all about a mad night out, the Castle is cool and airy and much more dignified. But it's grown on me.

The food is very nice – I recommend the fillet steak burger – and it's a comfortable and relaxing place to hang out. It gets too smoky sometimes, and I'm not keen on the gigantic wineglasses – unless you get a bottle of wine you feel like you've hardly got a mouthful in there. The wine list is very good, though, and they are about to start serving Leffe blonde beer according to a sign outside, so that gets a thumbs-up from me.

✎ *Amanda_Fuller, June 2005*

The Claret Free House

Addiscombe

5a Bingham Corner, off Lower Addiscombe Road, Addiscombe, Croydon, Surrey CR0 7AA

☎ 020 8656 7452

Excellent pub in an excellent position just a minute from the tram stop. A rare example of an old man's pub where young people aren't made to feel like criminals when they go in.

✎ *McDrunk, January 2006*

Great beer drinkers' pub. Small-looking frontage opens out into a long rectangular room, with the bar along the left-hand side. Mock Tudor decor looks a bit tacky in a building that clearly isn't very old, and the bar itself looks a bit like what you'd expect to find in the pool room of a nouveau riche celebrity's Essex manor house (exposed brickwork with a rustic wood structure above). However, you go to this place for the real ales, which are excellent. Six hand pumps: on my visit there was Shepherd's Neame Spitfire and Late Red, Dark Star Festival and Porter, Westerham SPA and Palmer's IPA. Prices range from £2.20 for session beers to £2.50 for premium beers. I gluttonously dived straight into the Dark Star Porter (ABV 5.5%) without sampling the Westerham SPA or Dark Star Festival first, but I'm a cask stout/porter fiend and just couldn't resist – it was lovely. The walls are adorned with nicely mounted old photographs of Croydon and brewery memorabilia.

The Claret is literally within a few yards of Addiscombe tram stop and well worth a diversion to make a visit. Along with the Beer Circus (massive selection of continental beers) and Royal Standard

(traditional boozer serving the Fuller's range), I'd rate the Claret as one of the best three pubs in Croydon and district.
✎ *Rich66, October 2005*

The Crown and Sceptre

South Croydon
32 Junction Road, South Croydon, Surrey CR2 6RB
☎ 020 8688 8037

One of those pubs where nothing much happens and nothing ever changes – that's a great thing.

Always friendly staff (low staff turnover, which is rare), consistently well-kept beers (both real ale and lagers), friendly regulars and quiet atmosphere conducive to good conversation.
✎ *lipster, February 2006*

Does what it says on the label. You can't really go wrong with Fuller's and this is a decent example deep in the swamplands of South Croydon. Nice food and bar staff too.
✎ *darloexile, May 2005*

The Dog and Bell

Deptford
116 Prince Street, London SE8 3JD
☎ 020 8692 5664

Beer in the Evening

Went for the pickle festival on Saturday. I have a deep love for this place.

✎ *MrScott, November 2005*

Great pub and friendly atmosphere. London Pride is my favourite and it's on tap all year round; also ESB. There are also the guest beers, which change every week or so. All food is cooked on the premises and is fantastic – not surprising as the new governor is a chef. Most of the customers are real-ale drinkers, not like certain people have said. The curry night was superb. Will be visiting more often from now on. Did I mention the barmaid was very nice ;-)

✎ *deptford_joe, November 2005*

Situated in an area into which anyone with any sense would not normally venture, the Dog and Bell is hardly a place you would find by accident. It is, however, well worth making an effort to visit. Winner of many CAMRA awards. They have three well-kept guest ales among the usual selection of lagers, cider, etc. The pub is quite spacious, clean and tidy, with a large side room and a small beer garden at the back. They also have one of the few remaining bar billiards tables (£1 a go). TV in the main bar but not really geared for sports (I actually watched an England game here and there were barely 20 people in the pub). Friendly and efficient staff. A bit of a gem in an area you would least suspect.

✎ *RogerB, September 2005*

Went in on Saturday night. It was quiet, which was fine by me, and the beer was delicious. A fine, fine place to have a chill and a natter with mates. The girl behind the bar was dead friendly and helpful.

✎ *MrScott, March 2004*

The Dog House

Kennington

Kennington Cross, 293 Kennington Road, Lambeth, London SE11 6BY
☎ 020 7820 9310

Good choice of beers and spirits, good music selection (very slightly unusual dance music mainly).

Staff are a bit laid back, so are the punters, and so is the decor :-)

Great relaxed atmosphere. My favourite pub by far in the area.
✎ *silverside, January 2006*

Seems to have improved recently, with staff much more responsive and bar manager friendly. However, still had to wait five-plus minutes at the bar to be served on a quiet Monday night. Still, mustn't grumble.

This is overall an excellent pub on your way to the excellent Indian restaurants on Kennington Road.
✎ *Anonymous, November 2005*

This is my other local, but I'd go out of my way for a drink here nevertheless. Great for watching the match, a quiet chat over some wine, or a raucous evening with friends.

Good collection of ancient board games too. West End prices, sadly, but very funky decor, which looks like it has grown on its own.
✎ *vinrouge, March 2005*

The Dulwich Woodhouse

Sydenham

39 Sydenham Hill, London SE26 6RS

☎ 020 8693 5666

☆ RAVE REVIEW

The Dulwich Woodhouse is unusual in several ways, not least in that it isn't quite in Dulwich. 'Sydenham/Crystal Palace/Dulwich borders Woodhouse' would be a more accurate but more cumbersome title. The pictures of the old palace on the wall give a clue to its own leanings though.

It's in a heavily wooded residential area, away from other shops and commercial premises. This gives the building and (large) beer garden a much more countrified feel than you'd expect from somewhere in Zone 3. It is served by decent bus routes (202, 356, 363, N63), so it isn't quite as remote as it looks on the map.

Ideal for a stroll up (and I do mean up – it's a steep hill) from Dulwich Village or Sydenham Hill Station on a weekend afternoon, this is a bright, welcoming semi-open-plan pub with tons of seats inside and out. The restaurant-style non-smoking area is literally a breath of fresh air from the main bar. Beer-wise, it's well-kept Young's, and they sometimes stock some of the brewer's more unusual draughts, such as the St George's summer ale. The bottled ale selection is worth noting if you want something different. The food is OK, with gastropub aspirations, but it'll hardly make Jamie Oliver quake in his boots. The staff are friendly and attentive and not overly aggressive when it comes to kicking out time (Wetherspoon pubs – take note please).

On the flip side from chilled afternoon boozing, I've had some big nights in here. From my recollection, the Saturday-night clientele seems a lot more young and attractive than the location would perhaps expect, although that was probably the (Young's) beer goggles.

✎ *Andrew Lipscombe (lipster), February 2006*

The George

Beckenham
111 High Street, Beckenham, Kent BR3 1AG
☎ 020 8663 1011

The only proper pub in Beckenham these days. If you like traditional pubs and decent beer, then it's well worth a visit.

✎ *FattusBlokus, February 2006*

Good old pub, this. Do enjoy it. Quite a cosy feel in the winter, with the nice big chairs and fire. In summer the beer garden is ace, so it has both markets covered. Can get very smoky on a busy night. The staff are excellent, always prompt and pleasant – apart from obviously having been told by the boss to ask routinely whether you want nuts or crisps after you've got your drinks – I'd ask for 'em if I wanted them! Good mixed crowd of people. Only letdowns are the Gents, which smell a bit, and the beer isn't the best I've ever had.

✎ *hazey, December 2005*

Excellent staff, terrific ales, comfy chairs, local cat that hogs the best seat by the fire. A more mature crowd tends to frequent, but there's more than enough cack kiddie pubs in Beckenham.

✎ *Bovine_Juice, December 2005*

The Golden Lion

Bexleyheath

258 Broadway, Bexleyheath, Kent DA6 8BE

☎ 020 8303 4268

Nice little pub to have a beer before moving on somewhere else. And they now sell Foster's!

✎ *Anonymous, December 2005*

The Lion is alright. Used to be more homely, but it's gone a bit 'wine bar' since they got new management. Fairly decent, though. Drinks aren't the cheapest, but they have a big screen for footy.

✎ *roryog, December 2005*

The Golden Lion. What can I say? How many times I have seen England lose in this pub? Such memories. Germany in '96. France and Portugal in '04. Argentina … Northern Ireland. If you want passion for an England game, this is the place! Bar staff are the nuts. Don't get in trouble. Bit chilly though.

✎ *cafc, November 2005*

The Greenwich Union

Greenwich

56 Royal Hill, London SE10 8RT

☎ 020 8692 6258

I shouldn't really like this pub – it doesn't serve bitter, it caters for families with kids, it's pretty pricey, and it's miles from where I live

– but I love it. It's the best pub in London. The beer's great, the staff are fantastic, and the atmosphere is always friendly. Treat yourself: go there!
✎ *Paintbrush, January 2006*

Excellent place. Young and enthusiastic barman took time to explain about the beer and offer samples while we tried to choose from the impressive array of delicious beers. Recommended.
✎ *mally, July 2005*

Originally the Fox and Hounds, the pub was given a facelift and a name-change to offer something different to it's next-door neighbour, the Richard I. It's very much a pub targeted at the ale connoisseur – those looking for something a bit different and a bit special. There's not much in the way of lager or alcopops, but that's not why you're there. It's the unique range of delicious beers that make this establishment rather unique.

The furniture is not the best, but the food is good and the bar staff are friendly and often offer a try before you buy on the various beers they have.
✎ *DJ.Alexander, April 2005*

I visited this pub for the first time yesterday and had a superb session. This is a very friendly and welcoming modern pub in the backstreets of Greenwich, offering the discerning drinker a wide range of beers from the Meantime brewery. Note: the cask ale on hand pump is brewed by Rooster's Brewery. The serious, discerning drinker is offered tasters before making his or her choice, which is very useful if you have not tasted the beers. Good food by day; excellent tapas by night. I found the place very friendly. The blonde girl who was always smiling came to see how we enjoyed our food and our beer, and the two guys behind the bar were helpful and efficient. I will go again. Recommended.

✎ *ladnewton, June 2004*

The Jolly Woodman

Beckenham

9 Chancery Lane, Beckenham, Kent BR3 6NR

☎ 020 8663 1031

Excellent pub. Great ales.

✎ *Bovine_Juice, December 2005*

Easily the best pub in Beckenham. Accommodating to all ages of drinkers and excellent ale. The new owners are apparently going to start work on the courtyard around the back.

✎ *Anonymous, October 2005*

Terrific little side-street local dating back to the mid-eighteenth century. In one of the oldest streets in Beckenham. The place is bursting with character. Not a lot of room inside, but the sheltered rear garden is perfect for a summer's afternoon whiling away a couple of hours.

One major plus point is that this is one of the only places in the borough I know of that serves a pint of the fantastic Caledonian Deuchars IPA, alongside Harveys Sussex and, at present, Gales Best Bitter. One criticism is that they should have a larger range of rare ales from microbreweries; then this would be an

almost faultless 10. Dartboard by the back door, friendly bar staff and I'm sorry, but even the outside toilet facilities I find endearing. Will definitely be returning.
✎ *young_camra_collectiv, August 2005*

I really like this pub – you'll almost certainly have to stand in the winter, but the beer garden is good and there's definitely something to be said for a pub that doesn't appear to have been refurbished in 40 years. Often serves Harveys Sussex Best, which is a lovely pint.
✎ *pubcollector, March 2005*

The Oakhill Tavern

Beckenham
90 Bromley Road, Beckenham, Kent BR3 5NP
☎ 020 8650 1279

Great character pub with good beer.
✎ *Bovine_Juice, December 2005*

Definitely the proverbial oasis in the Beckenham decent-pub desert. Looks lovely after a complete refurb. Good U-shape layout of seating around the bar, so even when it's busy you can have some privacy. Superb Sunday roasts and sizeable 'Oakhill-style' sandwiches keep bringing us back for more every weekend. Three fireplaces give the rooms an all-time welcoming warmth in winter, but the real hit is their gorgeous back garden in late spring/early summer – what better way to enjoy your Sunday lunch – or BBQ – than sharing a wooden table and a drink with your friends in the sun, surrounded by an abundance of colourful flowers and greenery

and listening to water slowly spilling from a fountain into their little pond? See you there.
✎ *Jet, March 2005*

The Plume of Feathers

Greenwich
19 Park Vista, London SE10 9LZ
☎ 020 8858 1661

Recently visited the park and museums so after splitting up this was the obvious place to reassemble. Good ales and friendly staff. It is dog-friendly as well, so you just have to be careful you don't kick over a water bowl and dampen the goods you've just bought in the market.
✎ *lout_from_the_lane, January 2006*

A great little pub. Friendly staff, good beer and really nice food. The kebabs are well recommended.
✎ *DJ.Alexander, August 2005*

Not far away from having everything: great beer, locals are friendly, bar staff pleasant and helpful, excellent food, pretty garden at rear. Also handy for Maze Hill Station. In short, all a good local should be. I wish I lived closer. Well done to all involved. Recommended.
✎ *mally, July 2005*

A beautiful pub – if you come from outside England and you want to experience a 'pub', come here as you will feel the atmosphere, the beer, the cosiness, the football. And the food's OK too.

Child-friendly, by the way, which is no bad thing given the nearby park.

✎ *georgebridges, January 2005*

The Portrait

Sidcup

7 Main Road, Sidcup, Kent DA14 6NF

☎ 020 8302 8757

☆ RAVE REVIEW

Most of our public houses have changed over the past few years and are becoming modern bars with restaurant menus, some of them purposely built or using large converted high-street premises. The Portrait is a perfect example of the latter, being a cleverly converted Victorian building opposite the police station on Sidcup's Main Road, with parking facilities behind in a council pay-and-display carpark.

Tom and Vee who manage the bar for the Barracuda Group are very experienced in the licensed trade, as is evident when you watch them work. But they are also very personable and remind me of the old-fashioned mine host style of landlord. As you would expect from such an experienced couple, the staff are very well trained, despite their young age (that might be me getting old), and polite. When not busy, they can be quite chatty as long as you're reasonably sober and compos mentis.

There is an excellent choice of beers, wines and spirits – so much so that even I, a committed Stella Artois drinker, have been tempted away from my regular brand on occasions to try some of the new seasonal ales or spirits on offer. The extensive menu changes frequently and there are always specials on offer, with at least one roast featured on a Sunday.

When all is said and done, as a drinker of several years' experience, I would heartily recommend the Portrait as one of the best among the myriad bars that populate South East London.

✎ *Stephen Batty (stephen.batty), December 2005*

The Prince Albert

Bexleyheath
2 Broadway, Bexleyheath, Kent DA6 7LE
☎ 020 8303 6309

This place hasn't changed in 20 years. Neither have the owners. I like it. Eagerly await a brass kettle landing on my head so I can sue 'smiley Ben' for every penny.

✎ *bigaerials, December 2005*

Shepherd Neame pub, so it has the obligatory list of excellent beers. The most entertaining thing here is the frankly ridiculous selection of brass pots, pans, jugs, ships' ornaments and God knows what else hanging from the seriously overstressed ceiling.

It gives the impression of drinking in a half-pub/half-antique shop environment. And oddly, that's a very good thing.

✎ *Beermeup, September 2005*

The Princess of Wales

Blackheath
1a Montpelier Row, London SE3 0RL
☎ 020 8297 5911

Excellent boozer with great range of beers. Friendly, helpful bar staff, which is a good thing given the state my companions and I were in after a 'Leo Sayer' a few weeks back. Also does a blinding (if a little pricey) breakfast.
✎ Boss_Hog, January 2006

This place seemed like three different pubs in one. By the front door it is fairly old-school and football-colours-friendly. As you move towards the back, it gets progressively posh, until you hit the well-heeled buggy brigade, especially on a Sunday afternoon. A pub that caters for everyone – what an amazing concept these days.
✎ cardamom, December 2005

The Ramblers Rest

Chislehurst
Mill Place, Chislehurst, Kent BR7 5ND
☎ 020 8467 1734

Excellent trad ale house midway between Chislehurst Station and town centre. Five ales, including Courage Best, Wells Bombardier, Greene King IPA and Brakspear Bitter, all perfectly preserved. Draught lagers include the lesser-spotted Beck's, alongside Foster's and 1664. Homemade mulled wine served around

Christmas. Two bars on two levels, with friendly, welcoming and accommodating bar staff, especially the landlord.

Almost impossible to find if driving. Accessible off Old Hill, down a long, winding, narrow drive with no signposts. However, this is probably best, as I'm sure you can imagine the carnage once the six-vehicle carpark becomes full. My suggestion: park on Old Hill near the Imperial Arms and walk through Mill Place and then left up the footpath towards the pub.

No reservations in saying this is the best pub in Chislehurst.
✎ *young_camra_collectiv, December 2005*

My favourite pub in Chislehurst. Not a huge selection of beer, but a nice place to arrange to meet up, and the garden is lovely in the summer.
✎ *Paulie, February 2005*

The Red Lion

Bromley
10 North Road, Bromley, Kent BR1 3LG
☎ 020 8460 2691

Excellent back-street pub. A proper pub. Five very well-kept real ales. Reasonably priced snacks. Well worth a visit.
✎ *longfella, December 2005*

Friendly and knowledgeable service. Ales always well kept and reasonably priced. Decent clientele. Simply what a pub should be.
✎ *sussexsketch, August 2005*

How have I lived in Bromley for 20 years without discovering this place? Well, probably because it's in a teeny tiny back street midway between Bromley North and Sundridge Park train stations. The best of at least three Greene King pubs within a half-mile radius (although you'd be forgiven for not knowing any of them existed). IPA, Abbot and Harveys Sussex always on, with quality guests rotating frequently. Check out the range of pump clips decorating the attractive dark wood bar. Not overly pricey, and a real suntrap of a front courtyard. Landlord highly knowledgeable on ales, which is always a bonus. A proper pub-goers' pub in the quiet, old part of Bromley town. 10/10.

✎ *young_camra_collectiv, May 2005*

This is a cracking little pub, a local tucked away in the side streets in Bromley North. It serves a good pint of Harveys and several other guests. It is small and gets crowded, but the atmosphere is always chatty and happy. No hormone-fuelled idiots here. Thoroughly recommended for a good beer with good company.

✎ *Get_me_some_Old_Tom, April 2005*

Richard I

Greenwich

52 Royal Hill, London SE10 8RT

☎ 020 8692 2996

Nice Young's establishment. Invaded by morris dancers while I was there but their accordion player was a nice change of pace. Good-looking food and I enjoyed my Young's bitter. Garden looked inviting.

✎ *jorrocks, October 2005*

Very good Young's beer, lovely garden, nicely tucked away from the towny commercial bit of Greenwich. Sat out on the street at the front and watched the world go by.

✎ *danrkelly, September 2004*

Cool pub, comfy and cosy, instead of grubby and scruffy. Big garden. Pint of Waggle Dance went down a treat.

✎ *MrScott, May 2004*

I've only been here once, on a beautiful spring afternoon. The Young's was delicious, and the garden was perfect for kicking back and talking. I had no problem with the staff, as they totally ignored the garden, so I could get my exercise stumbling back and forth to the bar. Not being from the area, the whole street was a nice surprise.

✎ *martineaux, August 2003*

The Robin Hood and Little John

Bexleyheath
78 Lion Road, Bexleyheath, Kent DA6 8PF
☎ 020 8303 1128

This is a classic back-street pub. Eight real ales on offer. Sadly I had time to get through only half the range, but every one was in excellent condition.

The pub is busy, but not crushingly so, the locals are chatty and polite, and the bar staff are brilliantly efficient. The wall of awards from CAMRA bears testament to this pub's excellence. A classic.

✎ *cackgsy, November 2005*

This wonderful little back-street local completely deserves all the awards it has won. A good range of real ales, all beautifully kept, a very friendly landlord and landlady, good food and a chatty and likeable clientele. Also a small but sunny and pretty beer garden for the warmer days. I would always recommend this pub to the real-ale drinker. By far the best pub in the area.

✎ *Get_me_some_Old_Tom, April 2005*

Good drinkers' pub and a great choice of hand-pump beers. Well worth a visit, so give it a try.

✎ *Anonymous, March 2005*

The Rosemary Branch

New Cross
44 Lewisham Way, London SE14 6NP
☎ 020 8692 2160

What a difference! A new manager and a new menu. The place could do with a new paint job, but the welcome you receive from the staff more than makes up for it. The food is highly recommended and portions are very large. I cannot fault the service or food. And spent a very nice Sunday afternoon there. The new manager and her staff made us feel very welcome.

✎ *HOPEDIXON, February 2006*

Now under new management (thank God!). I thought I'd give it a try. Glad I did – no more banging loud music. New manager has loads of ideas for the place. Food was great – massive amounts and hot. Good prices.

If you have been put of going in the past because of the reviews, then give it a go now.

✎ *rubywillow, January 2006*

The White Horse

Peckham Rye
20 Peckham Rye, London SE15 4JR
☎ 020 7639 1459

A great pub on a Saturday morning for chatting to the old boys of Peckham.(What they don't know about Peckham over the years isn't worth knowing.) Pub interior could do with a bit of brightening up, as it's a bit dingy, but still very friendly staff. Will go again.

✎ *landormick, January 2006*

The Sunday lunch at this pub is South London's best-kept secret. I challenge anyone to find a better, more-value-for-money Sunday lunch anywhere. The rack of lamb is to die for at a mere £6. Even the Yorkshire pudding is homemade.

It is a family-run pub and regulars are treated like VIPs. For the younger crowd, pop over the road to the Rye Hotel, which has a wonderful beer garden and is tastefully decorated, and there are friendly, chatty staff. The pubs in Peckham are really on the up. Also try the Gowlett – again, nice management and friendly staff – no TV screens blaring in the background, organic wines and delicious pizzas. Unfortunately, this is the only choice of food, which is why I would only give it an 8/10.

✎ *hooley, July 2005*

The William Camden

Bexleyheath

Avenue Road, Bexleyheath, Kent DA7 4EQ

☎ 020 8303 1420

Love this pub! Full of pleasant regulars. Staff are always really nice and friendly, particularly Pete, who is a complete diamond, and Ed, who is just a legend.

Great place for watching the footie or playing pool. Has the best karaoke nights and a good pub quiz on Sunday. It is well and truly the best place to be any night of the week.
✎ *lubyloo, January 2006*

Nice pub these days. Used to be a bit nasty, but they've turned it around. Best place for pool tables in Bexley. They have a decent selection of tipples and the staff are plenty nice.
✎ *roryog, December 2005*

My local pub and the best pub in Bexleyheath. Full of pleasant people, good pool players and the best beer for miles. It's got wicked doormen, brilliant and hard-working managers and the best staff around.
✎ *simon_barman, November 2005*

It's not a bad pub, especially for Bexleyheath – pool tables, big-screen football, Golden Tee, a Golden tee-style bowling game, quiz machine, choice of lagers. I like it.
✎ *ronnierosenthal, August 2004*

Zero Degrees

Blackheath
Montpelier Vale, London SE3 0TJ
☎ 020 8852 5619

Top-quality beer still the agenda here. Visited with two friends. Food very good, and we got a table within two minutes of walking in at 8 p.m., which was great. The pale ale and the black lager are the beers to go for.
✎ *ladnewton, December 2005*

Popped in here for a quick bite and beer with a group of friends. The bar area and microbrewery area are beautifully presented, although the downstairs eating area could do with some more attention, as it was very dull and fairly cheap looking. Upstairs was pretty nice and my pizza was lovely. The view was also nice. If you have a large group, make a booking – we could only get tables of four, so our group was spread over two separate tables.

They brew six beers here, and the friendly barman let us have a taste of them before selecting. The pale ale is an absolute winner. I'd definitely come back if I found myself in the area.

Oh yeah: four quality pints for under a tenner. Bargain!
✎ *chrisgill33, November 2005*

Great place for a night out in a big group. Unusual beers brewed on site in a large open-plan building almost resembling a warehouse. Restaurant-quality food is prepared on view in front of the bar. Metallic tables and chairs, both upstairs and down, giving it a modern trendy feel that some could misinterpret as feeling a bit cold.

Plaques explain the brewing process, and you can see how it's done from start to finish through huge windows behind the bar. The beers are then piped straight to the taps. The seasonal Mango wheat beer, was amazing but the pale ale and pilsner went down a treat too. Zero Degrees also does an unbeatable beer-and-pizza offer at lunchtimes that must be tried and is a great introduction to this stylish, twenty-first-century 'snooty' ale bar.

✎ *young_camra_collectiv, October 2005*

Amazing pear, gorgonzola and walnut pizza. Mussels are good too – you get plenty of chips and mayo to fill you up. Food is slightly changeable, depending on which chef is in charge of that cavern of a pizza oven. The microbrewed beer really is quite good. A bargain at £2.40 a pint. Nice huge glass etched diagrams all over the place to show you the science behind all the tuns and other stainless steel equipment that you can see way beyond the bar.

Grab one of the laminated drinks menus. I figure if you work your way through all the beers on the list, then you've earned it. Don't try to steal the glass etchings, though. That would be bad. They sell 50-litre kegs for around £70 too. If you've got your white van with you, you can take some of the fun home.

Little bit of seating outside for the summer, with good view of the heath and the church (if you like looking at buildings). Plenty of other things to look at in Blackheath, though, if you know what I mean.

✎ *daveboden, August 2005*

East

5b Urban Bar

Limehouse
27 Three Colt Street, London E14 8HH
☎ 020 7537 1601

This is the best bar that I know of in London, which I should be keeping quiet about because I've always preferred it when it's not busy. You can't just come in for one: it will suck you in and make you postpone your plans until tomorrow.

Something's always happening. The staff and owners are fantastic and make the atmosphere what it is. This is no theme bar: this is drinking for people who like it real and hardcore. Love it!
✎ *dan...rodney, December 2005*

The Grapes is my number-one local, but this place comes a close second, not least for being the 'anti-Grapes' :-) A very useful late licence and you never know quite what to expect in here.

Never a place for a quiet pint – in the best possible sense of course. The Leffe is evil, mind.
✎ *tim_eyles, November 2005*

The Angel

Rotherhithe

Bermondsey Wall East, London SE16 4NB

☎ 020 7394 3214

A great restoration has been done on this place. The no-smoking bar upstairs has a wonderful view of the river. Food is good, and there is a lot of it. Have had a couple of good sessions there.
✎ *jackthelad, November 2005*

As good a pint of Sam Smith's as you can get down south. Extensive refurb recently. Downstairs bar lovingly restored (see the beautiful terrazzo floor). Upstairs, breathtaking views of the river. Can't vouch for the grub as I haven't eaten here.
✎ *almost_an_old_git, November 2005*

The first thing to note is that this is a Sam Smith's pub. To some this means heaven (good beer at knockdown prices), but to others it means hell (crap beer at knockdown prices) ... and don't even mention the Sam Smith's cola. Personally I have no problem with Sam Smith's beers, the Cider Reserve is excellent, and I even like the infamous wheaty-tasting Man in the Box Ayingerbrau lager. So it's a good start for the Angel, apart from the fact that there are no beers on hand pump. Having reopened recently after a lengthy refurbishment, everything is gleaming and spotless, with several nautical themed pictures adorning the walls. From the central bar, two or three Victorian-style screens radiate, separating the pub into several smaller drinking areas. There are a few snugs for those who wish to get intimate over their pint. Upstairs is a quieter non-smoking room, and it is from here that the pub's greatest asset becomes obvious: the panoramic windows offer the legendary picture-post-card views of Tower Bridge – spectacularly illuminated at night. The Angel will probably appeal immensely to tourists, but for now it seems that just a privileged few are aware that it is once again up and running – well worth going out of the way for and idling some time watching the boats go by ... if you can stomach the Sam Smith's.

✎ *RogerB, October 2005*

The Approach Tavern

Bethnal Green
47 Approach Road, London E2 9LY
☎ 020 8980 2321

Brilliant pub. Good beers, excellent jukebox, good mix of people and you can almost always get a seat. Highly recommended.

✎ *SusanC, November 2005*

London's best pub? So very close. Without a doubt this place just oozes the type of local we all want deep down, whatever our age. Great beer, terrific food, friendly staff, and an atmosphere that is stunning – just leave by yourself with Dire Straits' 'Why Worry?' on your CD player.

✎ *TimJones, September 2004*

Victorian pub on a tree-lined avenue in Bethnal Green. Good range of beers and heated patio area at the front, behind railings. One of the cosier boozers left in the area.

✎ *danrkelly, May 2004*

The Birkbeck Tavern

Leyton

45 Langthorne Road, London E11 4HL

☎ 020 8539 2584

Really nice pub. Good beer, good staff, friendly to Leyton Orient and visiting football fans. A bit out of the way, but well worth looking for.

✎ *patrickjsm, December 2005*

Brilliant pub in Leyton back streets (you won't find it by accident), serving a good range of guest beers to a mix of locals and, on match days, a mix of home and away fans (never yet seen trouble). Warm, welcoming, unpretentious – basically everything a pub should be. Plus, last time I was in there, a beer-company rep was dishing out a free beer to everyone.

✎ *pablos13, September 2005*

On a hot and sweaty Sunday evening, this pub's garden is a gem. Three ales and all in good condition.

Nice place and only a short walk from Leyton Station.

✎ *M. Sticker, June 2005*

The Britannia

Barking

1 Church Road, Barking, Essex IG11 8PR

☎ 020 8594 1305

This is a most excellent pub, and the beer is always good. Comfortable old-style back-street pub with three bars. The licensee has been here for a long time and allows no antisocial individuals. Expect good food and good service here. It is a family pub with a great reputation. It certainly deserves the CAMRA 'Pub of the Year' certificates. Rita and John deserve a pat on the back for their hard work.

✎ *Beerbunter, September 2005*

Excellent beer and regularly wins CAMRA 'Pub of the Year' for the area. Haven't seen it crowded for years, but well worth a visit.

✎ *BusterGut, May 2005*

The Camel

Bethnal Green
277 Globe Road, London E2 0JD
☎ 020 8983 9888

Spent lunchtime here. Menu is pie and mash only, but good-quality pies. Will spend the next few weeks working through them all. Good wine list, and relaxed smoke-free atmosphere. Can recommend this recently opened pub.

✎ *Anonymous, January 2006*

Spent all of Sunday arvo in this recently renovated and reopened gem in the East End. It's smoke-free so blissful, and the pie selection was outstanding. Friendly staff, clean loos, nice interior. Will definitely be back. Only bummer was the music (a Tracy Chapman CD), but maybe they'll accept compilations from punters?

✎ *kabyar, December 2005*

The Captain Kidd

Wapping
108 Wapping High Street, London E1W 2NE
☎ 020 7480 5759

It's well off the usual track and worth a stop or going out of your way for, especially in summer, although the fixed picnic-table setup is a little impractical if there are more/less than four of you. The food is a little overpriced, especially being a Sam Smith's, but booze makes up for that. It's an extremely popular place for Antipodeans over the weekend for some reason.
✎ *cardamom, November 2005*

My local, and one of the best pubs in London. If you haven't been, go! Cheap beer, excellent staff, wonderful location, great atmosphere. Not touristy, but very popular with visitors when they find it.
✎ *Nailed, June 2005*

Best pub in the world, ever! Sam Smith's chain means its cheap and friendly. On the river with beer garden, so summer nights are excellent. Have had two birthday all-dayers in here, and the staff showed the patience of saints.
✎ *Dr_Cirrohsis, June 2005*

Lovely pub. Relatively recent conversion of old warehouse, but beautifully done.

Best time to visit is at dusk on a sunny day, when the sun bounces off the skyscrapers at Canary Wharf. Gorgeous.
✎ *tonyandrachel, January 2005*

The Chesham Arms

Homerton
5 Mehetabel Road, London E9 6DU
☎ 020 8985 2919

Very nice local pub. Worth a visit.
✎ *Anonymous, September 2005*

A gem of a pub, hidden away just off Homerton High Street, behind Sutton House. Good selection of beer, great friendly staff and locals.
✎ *marty21, December 2004*

The Cricketers

Woodford
299–301 High Road, Woodford Green, Essex IG8 9HQ
☎ 020 8504 2734

Nice old man's pub. Most expensive pub around the area, but well worth it.
✎ *Lembo, November 2005*

A *superb* session last night! I was there with a mate and had AK, Country and Strong Hart, all of which were in excellent condition. A good old pub singsong took place, here including some good voices. All in all, a superb virtually unspoilt traditional basic boozer.
✎ *ladnewton, December 2003*

The Dove

Bethnal Green
24 Broadway Market, London E8 4QJ
☎ 020 7275 7617

The Dove was included in our Regent's Canal pub crawl. We arrived on a sunny Wednesday afternoon and were greeted with a very large beer menu. I had a Belgian golden ale called Delirium Tremens – strong and refreshing taste. On a visit to London earlier, I also had the pleasure of enjoying the pub's food.
✎ *rune, November 2005*

My friend introduced me to this pub last summer and I was pleasantly surprised. The Dove is a great pub selling a fine selection of imported beers. The atmosphere was laid back and the food OK. It's now possible to get imported Belgian beers at your average local, but I've never seen this varied a selection outside a branch of Bierodrome (you have to try the strawberry beer).

If you fancy a chilled-out summer drink, you could do a lot worse than heading here. Another plus point is that across the street is the best pie-and-mash shop in the East End. Enjoy.
✎ *ganger, March 2005*

The Golden Grove

Stratford
146–148 The Grove, London E15 1NS
☎ 020 8519 0750

Good value for money, friendly hard-working staff. But like so many JDW pubs, something slows down the service, maybe because they take time with each customer – not sure about that one? Nice layout, with some booths inside, and a great garden with secluded tables. Oh, and the beer's well kept.

✎ *mikecharles_mjc, October 2005*

Great beers and friendly staff. I like the pictures on the walls, and there is even a history of Stratford. A good place to go when it's not busy.

✎ *peshwengi, April 2005*

Been going here now ever since it was converted by Wetherspoon from a shirt shop (Dickie Dirt's). Although it's seen better days, it still upholds the Wetherspoon traditions of no music, no pool, no Sky and loads of cask beer :-)

✎ *graley, December 2004*

The King Edward VII

Stratford
47 Broadway, London E15 4BQ
☎ 020 8534 2313

The area around Stratford shopping centre and the station is a William Hogarth print made into a film by David Lynch. With a bit of Hieronymus Bosch chucked in. This pub really is the only reason for going there. Well worth a visit if you happen to be in the area. If you sit in the windows at the front, you can watch the winos punching each other in the street.

✎ *Albert_Campion, December 2005*

Excellent pub with a selection of real ales (Adnams Broadside and Charles Wells Bombardier, among others). Used to be a great haunt of students of the nearby university, but probably less so now as the upper bar has been transformed into a fully fledged restaurant.
✎ *graley, January 2005*

The only reason to go to Stratford is for this pub. The rest of the place is like Rhyl on a bleak weekend. Thankfully, the Eddie manages to give some sort of hope for the residents and locals.
✎ *Anonymous, March 2004*

The North Star

Leytonstone
24 Browning Road, London E11 3AR
☎ 020 8989 5777

Discovered this one on Saturday by pure chance (due to 'house full' signs at the Sheepwalk's Saturday-night gig). What a wonderful gem of a pub! A real traditional two-bar local in the oldest surviving 'village' part of Leytonstone. Lovely atmosphere, friendly service, fascinating pictures and memorabilia around the walls, and three beers on top form – Deuchars IPA, Broadside and Bombardier. Top boozer.
✎ *E17Bee, January 2006*

This is a really good pub. It's on a lovely old street and you could almost imagine you were in a country village. When the sun's shining, it's hard to believe there's a McD's full of chavs a hundred yards away. Beer is kept well, and the staff and regulars are friendly. There's also a little beer garden out the back. Decor is pleasantly knocked about, with some lovely old tongue-and-groove. A great place to go while the girlfriend endures the horror that is Tesco.

✎ *Albert_Campion, November 2005*

This is one of very few pubs today that has an incredibly friendly and a real family feel about it. Fairly small compared with pubs on the high street, which makes it the first choice when there are only two to four of you. Music rocks and accessible dartboard.

✎ *JamesDaff, November 2005*

The Old Globe

Stepney
191 Mile End Road, London E1 4AA
☎ Telephone 020 7790 3524

Nice to see the pub getting good reviews. Let me tell you, boys and girls, this pub was probably the busiest pub in the East End bar none in the late 1970s to late 1980s. This pub was sardines Thursday to Sunday. There were a few others equally like it – the Rose and Punch Bowl, Carpenters Arms, Jug House, Prince Regent, to name but a few. Those were the days. You don't know what you missed.

✎ *moncrief, January 2006*

This has to be my favourite pub in the country. Beer always in good shape. A good rotation of real ales. Interesting locals. A DJ playing decent old-time rock 'n' roll with some 1980s' stuff thrown in for good measure. Best of all, no bloody chavs!

✎ *Zaphod, March 2005*

The Palm Tree

Mile End
Haverfield Road, London E3 5BH

Strolling along Regent's Canal, we had a beer break at the Palm Tree in Mile End Park. A public house from the 1930s with heavy curtains at the windows. Nice decoration with china and flowers. Friendly reception and a few real ales in perfect condition. Music from Michael Bublé in the background. Three palm trees outside the pub.
✎ *rune, November 2005*

Can't agree more with comments posted so far – an oasis in what is a desert for decent non-theme pubs. Good service, good beer, good luck to 'em.
✎ *chippysupper, December 2004*

Blimey – and I thought the good old East End boozer had died with the encroachment of the poncy gastro pubs. Went there last night to find myself caught up in the midst of a Christmas knees-up – carols and good cheer aplenty. I have only lived in the vicinity for a couple of months but in that time have managed to visit the majority of pubs in the area and this is by far the best, mainly because it has so much character, something often lacking these days. Would recommend it to anyone – especially on a Saturday night, when the aging crooners take a turn on the mic.
✎ *katya_1978, December 2004*

Best boozer in London! Amazing wallpaper, and fantastic OAP jazz band to boot. A real treasure.
✎ *Anonymous, January 2004*

The Pembury Tavern

Hackney
90 Amhurst Road, London E8 1JH
☎ Telephone 020 8986 8597

I went last night. Good to see real cider available in another London pub. Very friendly, knowledgeable staff.
✎ *tharg, January 2006*

I visited the pub for the first time last night. A very impressive bank of hand pumps. The Jack O'Legs by Tring was my pick of the evening. The pub seems perfectly suited to beer festivals and it would be wonderful to see it crammed full of people. My only very slightly negative comment is that I would have chosen a darker colour for the walls. The light colour makes the place appear vast and a bit too bright.
✎ *salamanda, January 2006*

Welcoming BITE users to the Pembury, which opened last Friday to fill an enormous gap in East London's real-ale map. It was a privilege to attend the opening night. Clean, bright and spacious, and yet welcoming, the Pembury Arms will offer drinkers a completely non-smoking environment in which to enjoy up to 16 real ales. The pub occupies a corner property and has a slightly L-shaped interior. Large rectangular tables are useful for groups of about six to eight people. A kitchen is on the way, and is scheduled to come into operation in the summer. This pub deserves to succeed. Anyone visiting will see the effort and energy that has been expended in its renaissance, and it ought to be seen as a trailblazer for future pubs. Excellent!
✎ *ladnewton, January 2006*

The Plough

Walthamstow
173 Wood Street, London E17 3NU
☎ 020 8503 7419

Great little boozer serving a good variety of well-kept beer. Friendly punters and plenty of entertainment throughout the year. Well worth a visit if you haven't been there before.
✎ *3DoorsDown, February 2006*

Excellent house – good beer kept well, friendly atmosphere, wide range of music, comedy, etc., in back room. A gem. Now why can't we have a pub this good in central Walthamstow?
✎ *E17Bee, September 2005*

The Prospect of Whitby

Wapping
57 Wapping Wall, London E1W 3SH
☎ 020 7481 1095

Yarrr me mateys, best pirate pub in town! Great food, good booze selection and ideal surroundings. Now if only they'd get some more ciders on tap, I'd never leave.
✎ *maddiekat, January 2006*

'Er indoors and myself stopped off in the Prospect after she had dragged me around London all afternoon sightseeing, etc. What a nice place. Friendly and attentive staff, good beers and an ambience that isn't found too often any more in many boozers. Sank a couple of beers and had some excellent food – the deep-fried brie is just great! Not a tourist in sight by the way – just some regulars having a yarn over a load of beers by the sound of them. Give the place a try – you won't be disappointed.

✎ *harlequin, September 2005*

The best pub in Wapping. Great Guinness and decent regulars make this a real local rather than the bar/tourist traps that have overrun the surrounding areas. Unfortunately, Chris is about to leave as landlord. No doubt the coaches will continue unabated. Consistently perfect for a chilled pint, whether mid-summer/inter. No TV. Joy! Lovely views of the river. Food is good for the money. Enjoy.

✎ *smiley, February 2005*

The Prospect – what can you say about London's oldest riverside pub that a thousand tourist guide books have not already said? Well, Chris – best landlord in England; beer – best it's been in years; wine – well, they have three New Zealand wines, which is fine by me; and food – well, 150 times better than when I worked in the kitchen.

Great views, long nights and sometimes a magical atmosphere.

✎ *TimJones, September 2004*

The Queens Arms

Walthamstow
42 Orford Road, London E17 9NJ
☎ 020 8520 6760

Without a doubt, this is the finest pub in the village. Wonderful characters in front of and behind the bar. A splendid selection of intoxicating liquor.

And definitely the best DJ in Waltham Forest. This is a proper pub and really refreshing for anyone that's ever had the misfortune to suffer the sterile environments that the Nags Head and the Castle have to offer.
✎ *Lord_bangstick, December 2005*

Great pub. Had a fantastic night on Friday. Bar staff are gorgeous and know their stuff. Pub was very busy but they served everyone with a smile on their face. Thoroughly recommended.
✎ *jedibond, May 2005*

The Spotted Dog

Barking
15 Longbridge Road, Barking, Essex IG11 8TN
☎ 020 8594 0228

Easily the best pub in Barking. Been coming here for years before and after West Ham's games (always busy on match days). Shame the sawdust has gone. Big pub with loads of room to sit, including non-smoking area.

Only letdown is variation of decent beer (by the way, Old Wallop isn't just Directors: it's been spiked with port – great if you fancy getting wasted).
✎ *tonymontana, February 2006*

This is by far the best pub in Barking. Lots of little nooks and crannies and also very spacious. Bit disappointed that they don't have the sawdust on the floor any more.

✎ *dgriffin, October 2005*

The best pub in Barking town centre, without doubt.

✎ *BinBagBob, February 2005*

The Three Colts

Buckhurst Hill

54 Princes Road, Buckhurst Hill, Essex, IG9 5EE

☎ 020 8506 0335

Great little country pub within five minutes' walk of a Tube station (can't think of many pubs that would fit that description). Has excellent real ale, a beer garden, a pool room, and just a small scattering of locals to make for a very relaxing evening. The antithesis of the orange MG-driving Chigwell brigade Blue Monday on Queen's Road.

✎ *drbee, December 2005*

The Travellers Friend

Woodford Green

496–498, High Road, Woodford Green, Essex IG8 0PN

☎ 020 8504 2435

Lovely little pub with many of its original features still intact. Friendly regular crowd and the staff and landlord were very

pleasant indeed. Beer is kept very well, with a choice of three lagers and usually five real ales. Good write-up in the *Good Beer Guide* too. Will definitely visit more often.
✎ *Rah_24, November 2005*

Very traditional. Unspoilt by Plc. A good range of real ales – five when I visited. Roaring fire and friendly locals. Mostly frosty staff, but one stood out as friendly.
✎ *graley, December 2004*

The Waltham Oak

Walthamstow
757 Lea Bridge Road, London E17 9DZ
☎ 020 8556 2460

Got a very good review in the local paper this week, and apparently has Young's Special on hand pump.
✎ *E17Bee, February 2006*

Wow! What a transformation! Definitely the best pub in Walthamstow. Beautiful interior – lovely leather sofas. We got two great steaks (buy one, get one free) and a one-litre carafe of wine for £15!
✎ *Juancoffee, January 2006*

Pub now reopened as the Waltham Oak (owned by the Big Pub Company). Looks quite flash inside when viewed from the bus.
✎ *E17Bee, December 2005*

The William IV and Sweet William Micro Brewery

Leyton

816 High Road, London E10 6AE
☎ 020 8556 2460

Generally speaking, the ales are consistently well kept, with Fuller's ESB, London Pride and Discovery usually available. The atmosphere is different, depending on whether it's a major match night, music or no special events. Events are well-notified, so it's easy to adjust the times of your visit depending on what you're looking for.

The back room has space for quite large parties. The clientele is varied, with quite a few regular groups and individuals. Like others, I hope the Sweet William Brewery is reopened. Its London Mild was a triumph. As to the bar staff, like with most pubs, treat them with respect and friendliness and you'll find those qualities returned. As a regular re-visitor, by choice, I take my money where I prefer to slake my thirst. There are other excellent pubs in the area, but I rate this one very highly.
✎ *mikecharles_mjc, October 2005*

Pub is now much better. Real ales whittled down to Fuller's (plus occasional guest) but kept in decent nick. Still a wide mix of punters, pleasingly cluttered decor, papers to read and friendly atmosphere. Put it this way: I regularly get a bus over here from the far side of Walthamstow rather than drinking in Walthamstow itself.
✎ *E17Bee, September 2005*

The Bank of Friendship

Highbury
224 Blackstock Road, London N5 1EA

In terms of service, this is the best pub in Highbury on match days. Queues three-deep at the bar are handled quickly and correctly, and you (normally) get change from a fiver for two pints :-) The pub's a bit small, which makes it awkward for watching the lunchtime games before going off to the Arsenal, but that's just nitpicking. I've never eaten in here but would like to one day. 8/10.
✎ *AshingdonMan, January 2006*

Brilliant pub! My local for many years. Just a nice place where you can enjoy a good ale (London Pride always on good form). Cosy without being poky or dingy. The type of pub that has become all too rare in Islington.
✎ *OldRogue, November 2005*

My local during the football season. The best boozer within a mile radius of AFC. My friends and I go there for the excellent beer (the Courage Best is very good, as is the Guinness) and the beer garden out the back. They have Sky TV, but because it's small inside watching can be cosy. Nonetheless a very fine boozer.
✎ *Mike_McCabe, July 2004*

The Boogaloo

Highgate

312 Archway Road, London N6 5AT

☎ 020 8340 2928

A small pub with some great live acts, apparently including such names as Coldplay (in their earlier days) and Babyshambles, although I'm still unsure whether Pete Doherty is a particularly good feature in your pub. It has a good jukebox and a great atmosphere the few times I have been there.

✎ *rl3_hill, December 2005*

Not bad at all. Weren't too many people around on a Saturday afternoon/evening, but a friendly waitress and a good drink. If you sit at the end of the seats facing Archway, and there's no one else in the pub, you get a good view of Suicide Bridge and St Paul's Dome. So there.

✎ *keep_it_green, April 2005*

Splendid place, this. Lovely atmosphere and friendly staff, and an excellent jukebox to boot. The DJ on the one time I was in on a Saturday went a bit overboard with the volume – it's only a wee pub mate! – but then again, I am an old git.

✎ *cid, February 2005*

I went there one night recently, and there was Frank Sinatra duetting with Edith Piaf, accompanied by Louis Armstrong, Charlie Parker and the bloke who plays piano in Casablanca. Seriously, it's a great pub, with a great jukebox (currently chosen by Bernard Butler), and with the best-organised music quiz in London.

✎ *billiliu, May 2004*

BRB at The Gate

Alexandra Park
Station Road, London N22 7SS
☎ 020 8889 9436

Marvellous little pub opposite Ally Pally train station that has the unusual advantage of an in-house pizzeria. Drinks are more expensive than anywhere else in this neck of the woods, but they do offer some fine draughts, an impressive selection of bottled beers and even some pretty decent cocktails. Bar service isn't for the impatient but is assured and efficient when it finally arrives. The regulars seem very tolerant of infrequent and first-time visitors, which always helps a place. The background music is surprisingly eclectic, with something for more or less everyone being played if you stick around long enough.

The food is exceptional and not badly priced either. If you are in a group of four or more, I recommend the following tactic: Whoever gets a round in orders a pizza as well and you share it when it comes, repeating the process when every member of your party's turn to buy a round comes. By the end of the evening you'll have each eaten roughly a whole pizza but had many different toppings and not stuffed yourself all at once.

Run by the same company behind the equally splendid Junction pub near Highbury and Islington Tube station.
✎ *Mr.Monkfish, December 2005*

I have recently moved into the area (Bounds Green) and having passed this pub several times on my way to Alley Pally I decided to go there yesterday with a friend. I'm glad that I did. The pub sells a limited selection of beers, but who cares when they serve Erdinger on draught. The decor is stripped-down wood (almost Hoxton trendy) and the atmosphere is laidback.

The wood-fired pizzas are inexpensive and tasty. The only complaint I've got is that at first the bar service was a little slow, but it soon picked up when the Obi-Wan Kenobi look-alike went upstairs for a break and two girls replaced him. All in all, a relaxed afternoon was spent there and I came away looking forward to returning soon.

✎ *ganger, May 2005*

The Camden Head

Islington

2 Camden Walk, London N1 8DY

☎ 020 7359 0851

Still drawn back to this place time after time, latest being last weekend. More of the usual really – standing room only and average drinks, disappointingly slow service this time, but maybe just a one-off.

✎ *Madcap, January 2006*

They have some decent real ales on here. I think you can get Broadside, Deuchars and a guest – or was Deuchars the guest? Can't remember. Anyway, it's a busy old gin palace given the soul-destroying once-over by a pubco. Seems to attract a – shall we say – less well-heeled patron, but maybe it's all the better for it.

✎ *Stonch, January 2006*

Warm pub with character. Food looked good and very reasonable. Check out two meals for £5.99.

✎ *lordhicks, January 2005*

The Catcher in the Rye

Finchley
317 Regents Park Road, London N3 1DP
☎ 020 8343 4369

One of the nicest pubs in central Finchley. Leather sofas, candlelight and an open fire generate a cosy atmosphere. Not surprisingly, therefore, the clientele when we visited were mostly couples and small groups. The beer selection is reasonable – all the usual suspects plus a couple of cask ales (John Smith's and Courage Best when we were there). The wine list looked satisfactory too. We didn't eat, though the food did look inviting, and there were some very tempting bar nibbles on display.

For sporting fans, football is shown on the plasma screen in the rear section of the pub.

✎ *Anonymous, January 2006*

Wow! What a place. We love it. Great lunch menu. Staff are really nice and friendly. They have a wonderful fireplace with couches around it. Have found my new local.

✎ *Bewitched, January 2006*

Unbelievable transformation – this is how a proper gastropub should look. The seating areas are split between warm comfortable leather couches in elegant colours in front of the two fireplaces and bistro-style tables on the raised areas. New wooden floors, cool rock-star photography and an industrial-style bar make this a very attractive place to go out in Finchley.

✎ *Jet, March 2005*

Crown and Horseshoes

Enfield

12–15 Horseshoe Lane, Enfield, Middlesex EN2 6PZ

☎ 020 8363 1371

Fantastic summer pub. A beer garden so big you could play cricket in it. Small inside, but comfortable. Prices aren't great, but I've seem worse, much worse.

✎ *stringerdax, August 2005*

One of my favourite pubs in Enfield. It probably has the largest garden of all the Enfield pubs. Even good in the winter, when the garden is not being used much. It now has two pool tables, in very good order too. It has a couple of fruit machines (25p machines, £25 jackpot) and a multigame video-quiz machine. Food is good. Nice selection of real ales, but not looked after well. The only niggle was that recently, on one of the hottest days of the year, they had only two bar staff on and the wait to be served was about half an hour at the bar.

✎ *JazHaz, August 2005*

Used to be a regular here throughout the 1990s but was driven away by the ridiculously inflated prices and the complacency of the management, which meant that the pub had gradually deteriorated from a lovely place for a drink and one of the best pubs in Enfield to being a place that my friends and I consciously avoided. I am very pleased to say that these problems have now been addressed and the pub is once again a good place to head for on an evening out. Bar staff are friendly and quick, and the whole place has had a lick of paint and new furniture and carpets, etc., which has improved the environment immeasurably. Prices have come down to a reasonable level and the choice of drinks has improved, as has the quality. Food is approachable, if nothing special, and a little bit steep. Now has decent TVs for watching sport and pool tables if you are bored. Beer garden is still the largest and best of its kind for miles around. Great location and at last the owners are making the most of it. Highly recommended. May well become a regular haunt again.

✎ *Mr.Monkfish, May 2005*

The Drapers Arms

Barnsbury

44 Barnsbury Street, London N1 1ER

☎ 020 7619 0348

It's well worth seeking this one out to spend a few relaxing hours drinking here during the afternoon. The perfect place for a quiet read, supping decent guest ale. It's a friendly pub and is located on quite possibly the finest street in London if you're into unspoilt historical urban residential architecture. The food here is pricey but renowned to be extremely good. Evening Standard Pub of The Year 2003.

✎ *PieFace, August 2005*

A friendly, efficient gastropub with reasonably priced good-quality food. Try the burger! Up to three real ales on hand pump, plus a good selection of foreign beers. The food is popular evenings and Sunday lunchtimes, so booking is wise. Ideal for a lazy afternoon. The rear of the pub features sofas and low tables. The pub is fairly down to earth and unpretentious. Recommended.

✎ *ladnewton, February 2004*

The Drum and Monkey

Archway
86 Junction Road, London N19 5QZ
☎ 020 7281 2414

I used to drink here in the late 1990s when I was a bus driver from the garage across the road in Pemberton Gardens. Entertaining pub full of friendly locals who like to have a sing-along when the karaoke is on. The pub is on Junction Road, Archway, which is a bit of a rough area but you'll always feel safe and welcome here. It's a shame that when the gentrification spreads to this area from Kentish Town, this pub might not last for too long and might be replaced by a chain pub. So get down there now before the Drum disappears forever. P.S. all bus drivers – me included – only drink after finishing their shifts.

✎ *ganger, March 2005*

A little gem of a pub. Good service and all round very friendly. Landlord Niall is good for laugh, even if he supports Man U. If you fancy a quiet pint on occasion, then this is the place to go. Well worth dropping into for a drink if you're passing – probably end up there all night!

✎ *wmon, February 2005*

I won't beat about the bush: I was absolutely terrified when I walked into this place. It looks exactly how a pub should look – threatening and gloomy. However, decent beer, decent prices, good bar staff and not even a shred of false pretence means that this pub just keeps getting better. It's how pubs should be.

✎ *Slipperduke, February 2004*

Good solid pub, with no mockney twats. A comfortable place to spend an evening.

✎ *grapat, March 2003*

The Duchess of Kent

Barnsbury
441 Liverpool Road, London N7 8PR
☎ 020 7609 7104

A lovely pub – classy but not pretentious, friendly and chilled. A great place to just relax and unwind, especially on Sunday afternoons. Staff are friendly and professional. The decor is stylish but not over the top. The food is also very good quality. Highly recommend this pub.

✎ *intermelocal, October 2005*

Great local. Outdoor seating provided and a large non-smoking dining area and use of games.

Never gets too busy and the food is great. Will be Jo Smith's new favourite.

✎ *bron1allen, June 2005*

The Elephant Inn

North Finchley

283 Ballard's Lane, London N12 8NR

☎ 020 8445 0356

Fuller's beer, a roaring log fire and comfy leather couches – this is definitely our favourite pub in the area.

✎ *Anonymous, January 2006*

A cracking Fuller's local, great range of beers and a lovely ambience. Some complain of its name change from the Moss Hall Tavern, but never mind – it's the best bet in North Finchley for a drink and a chat without loud music and the beer-boy crowd.

✎ *OldRogue, January 2006*

New to the area and went into what I thought was a private party – it wasn't. Excellent night with excellent DJs – one did an excellent Elvis takeoff. Friendly staff and not a sign of trouble.

✎ *FISHTHEMOD, November 2005*

This pub is magic! One bar is quiet and friendly; one bar is a bit louder and has a big screen for footy.

The beer is kept well, the bar staff are great, and Lucy, the new manager, is an absolute star. The regulars are friendly, and I have never had a bad night in here. It's one of those places where you pop in for a swift one and stay all night. There is also a great Thai restaurant upstairs, and an excellent quiz on a Monday.

✎ *vic_of_india, December 2004*

The Faltering Fullback

Finsbury Park
19 Perth Road, London N4 3HB
☎ 020 7272 5834

Can be overcrowded, but that's the price paid for a good atmosphere. The jukebox is cracking, but unfortunately your choices often cannot be heard in the aircraft hangar attached to the main pub. The Thai food is generally good. On balance, I like it as it's a good place to meet friends, particularly in the garden on a summer's evening, and looks like a magic pub from the outside.
✎ *dawnage, May 2005*

I've been to the Faltering Fullback several times in the last year and it is without doubt the best pub in Finsbury Park. True, the large room at the back does come across as a student union bar, but so what? There is a small beer garden that is open in the summer months, but because of its size it does get a little cramped. The best thing about this pub is the great horseshoe bar at the front, which serves good beer and food. But because of its popularity it is recommended to get there early if you want a seat. A great pub for summer evenings.
✎ *ganger, March 2005*

The Ferryboat Inn

Tottenham Hale
Ferry Lane, London N17 9NG
☎ 020 8493 9341

What a marvellous pub! There's nothing like it in the area. Great food and large open wood-burning fires in the winter.

✎ *paulmartin, February 2006*

If you live in the area, this is the place to go for a classic Sunday lunch. Good selection of beers, and the beer garden is essential on a balmy summers evening.

✎ *ganger, May 2005*

The Harringay Arms

Crouch End

153 Crouch Hill, London N8 9QH

☎ 020 8340 4243

This is possibly the best pub in London. It has the right criteria to be called a pub and not full of designer-perfumed clientele like the All Bar Pitcher and Piano opposite. Don't come in here for your Rioja or Chablis or toasted paninis with sea cress. The ales are great and not your usual watery London offerings. A real boozer for real unpretentious people.

✎ *Ale Bloke, December 2005*

A great pub with a really difficult quiz. The staff are friendly and efficient and it's easy to relax there. I also like the variety of age groups who drink side by side. This is also a good place for spotting the stars: I've seen EastEnders' Minty, Sean Hughes and Sergeant Boyden from The Bill (although not all together) there. Primetimetastic!

✎ *dawnage, May 2005*

A fine and decent traditional pub. No pretensions, good beer and friendly staff. Definitely an after-work-with-the-*Evening-Standard* pub. Relaxed and sound clientele.

✎ *keep_it_green, April 2005*

Great proper boozer hidden round the corner from Nat West. Highly recommended if you prefer conversation to shouting in dull chain pubs.

✎ *DKavanagh, December 2004*

The Island Queen

Islington

87 Noel Road, London N1 8HD

☎ 020 7704 7631

Made the trip here for the first time tonight after hearing good things. Very pleased I did. This pub applies the same formula as the Crown Tavern on Clerkenwell Green, the Castle at Farringdon and the Crown and Sceptre in Fitzrovia – Victorian pub with a scruffy makeover, retaining original features beneath a muted paint job. Great, great beer selection.

The differences between this pub and the others mentioned above seem to be wonderful service (ever-smiling barmaid twice came to our table to ask whether we wanted more drinks) and the fact that they do properly kept real ales (Pride, Deuchars IPA and Landlord). First impressions – a great pub. I will be going back on Sunday to try out the roast.

✎ *Stonch, January 2006*

A really good mixture of modern approach – draught continental beer as well as English and unusual menu – but in a traditional setting beautifully decorated. Service friendly and unhurried rather than slow, and lots of room for big parties and spaces for the more private to sit.

✎ *amleyland, November 2005*

If you're in Islington, give this place a visit – it's stunning and idiosyncratic and has a nice vibe to it.

✎ *cider_murray, July 2005*

Very handsome Victorian interior: high ceiling, lots of mirrors and windows, big wooden bar. Two real ales, comfortable, traditional and slightly shabby. I liked it a lot.

✎ *Anonymous, March 2005*

A true example of a traditional London pub. Its ornate features create a time warp to the turn of the century, and the beer is absolutely excellent: The Timothy Taylor Landlord was exquisite last night, for example.

Food is served but I didn't get the chance to try any. This is a back-street gem, and I recommend a visit as part of a good canal-basin crawl.

✎ *ladnewton, December 2004*

The Jorene Celeste

Islington
153 Upper Street, London N1 1RA
☎ 020 7226 0808

Overall I was impressed. A cavernous interior was a welcome relief once we got inside and the fact that I ran into an old friend here out of the blue always helps. Found it a little on the pricey side but given we were on rounds of doubles at this point perhaps I was just the unlucky one!

✎ *Madcap, January 2006*

Unusually decked out, with huge space put to good use, and paintings galore adorning the walls. This is an excellently chilled venue, with massive sofas, antique tables and chairs, plenty of room to move around, especially if you're with a group of friends. This place used to be the Royal Mail (a postman's pub), and it was great then.

It's probably the only pub that's undergone a transformation that I like. It definitely has improved. Apart from the name that is. If you look at the pub sign outside, the face does indeed have an uncanny resemblance to that odd-bod Boy George. It's a welcoming place for a quiet drink on your own, or with a group.

✎ *cider_murray, July 2005*

Good pub, chilled music and relaxing decor. Get a sofa at the back if you can and settle in for the evening. Perfect!

✎ *mattyd, July 2004*

I love this pub. The atmosphere is just right. The staff are always friendly and efficient.

There's an impressive selection of fine single malts behind the bar. But best of all is the delicious and very reasonably priced food. Easily my favourite London pub.

✎ *Anonymous, March 2004*

The Kings Head

Enfield

Market Place, Enfield, Middlesex EN2 6LL

☎ 020 8366 9381

⭐ **RAVE REVIEW**

The Kings Head is one of Enfield's longest-established pubs and has a prime location at the rear of the historic market square within a minute's walk of one of Enfield's stranger claims to fame: the Barclay's Bank that was home to the world's first cash machine.

It's a beautiful building with character and decorative windows and has long been worth a visit for this reason alone. Until recently, however, the pub was guilty of squandering its opportunity to be the best pub in the town centre as successive previous managers obviously felt that the exterior appearance entitled them to put in no effort whatsoever to make the pub a worthwhile destination for a pint or six.

At last, though, things have changed. Inside you'll find a nice relaxed and cosy atmosphere. The fairly dim lighting helps to make this large building still feel intimate and the good solid old-fashioned bar furniture is designed specifically to make you settle in for the evening. The bar staff are all very friendly, chatty and helpful, and there are normally enough on duty at any given time to ensure that there is never more than a couple of minutes' wait for service. The range of drinks is above average in comparison with other pubs nearby: as well as three or four lagers and a range of wines and spirits, there are normally a couple of guest ales to supplement the usual ales and bitter. The prices are remarkably cheap for a proper (i.e. non-discount pub chain) pub and the quality is always high. Food is also reasonably good but very much of the factory-produced-then-reheated-on-site variety, but at least it isn't overpriced.

Entertainment consists largely of background music, though there are a couple of small TVs around and a games room upstairs, with a couple of pool tables and a dartboard. The games room is a little dilapidated in comparison with the rest of the pub, but it is worth a quick visit just to enjoy the view from the window across the market square to the main road. Occasionally they have a quite challenging quiz evening as well. All in all, the thing that makes this place work is the clientele. It's not a place for the rowdy or overly trendy, and it attracts the kind of people that enjoy a good drink while chatting with friends and having a laugh, regardless of their age or social standing. There is never any trouble, which is more than can be said for most of the Enfield town centre pubs, and the regulars are a friendly bunch.

For Enfieldians like myself who actually still love the old place, the experience of walking out of here on a cold winter night over Christmas and New Year to be greeted by the sight of snow falling on the market square and the seasonal lights on the shops across the street with this lovely pub building behind you is one that brings a warm glow to your heart.
✎ *Scott Allin (Mr.Monkfish), February 2006*

Probably the best pub in Enfield – and the most civilised. The atmosphere is cosy with low lighting, almost like a Dutch brown cafe. The Tuesday quiz is something of an institution.
✎ *crimsonpirate, August 2005*

The Maid of Muswell

Muswell Hill

121 Alexandra Park Road, London N10 2DP

☎ 020 8365 4851

The Maid appears to have changed her clothes since my last visit there in Jan '04. Then it was a straightforward, no-nonsense, five-pints-of-lager-and-footie-on-screen boozer. Eighteen months on and the ugly duckling is not so ugly any more and is now a bit more fitting for such a well-to-do area. The patio outside now looks very smart, with a wicker fence and potted plants. Inside has been transformed with a more upmarket customer base in mind. It still retains some of the original stripped-back features and bare floorboards, but these now blend in with a mix of seating styles, potted plants and subtle lighting.

The bar staff were very welcoming and the well-kept beers include London Pride and Marston's Pedigree. Unfortunately, it would appear that the change has come at a price – £2.90 for a pint of Addlestones Cider compares badly with the £2.70 a pint I pay in Central London. But if this is your local, then you can probably afford it. The Maid won't be everyone's cup of tea, but there is little competition in the area. Handy for Alexandra Palace five minutes' walk up the hill.

✎ *RogerB, November 2005*

I stumbled (literally!) across the Maid a couple of months back and have been a regular visitor ever since. It's a lovely pub. It is clean and tidy, it has a good range of beers available (including strawberry beer – a favourite of my housemate) and the staff are always friendly. A good wine list and menu – the food is good – and a BBQ in the summer. Little bit pricey but it's Muswell Hill – what do you expect?

✎ *MikeyBee, August 2005*

The Mucky Pup

Angel
39 Queen's Head Street, London N1 8NQ
☎ 020 7226 2572

The pub is neat and cosy, with the landlord making sure that the place is snug during the crap weather that seems to be of late. I regularly pop in for the free wi-fi and a sizzling steak sandwich – the smell and taste are delish!

✎ *Anonymous, January 2006*

Heard about this place from friends who had sampled the huge Sunday dinners and been to the excellent Wednesday quiz night. Had the steak and ale pie, which was homemade and tasted superb. Spoke to the owners who run the place themselves and really add the personal touch, making everyone feel welcome. By the way, check out the beer garden and the world's biggest puppy (probably!).

✎ *Anonymous, April 2004*

This pub is chilled, with good beer and food. Massive pup called Iggy wanders the bar and the owners really make you feel welcome. A real treat.

✎ *scareyd, April 2004*

This pub has, after one visit, become my favourite boozer in Islington. Not only because I fell in love with Iggy the dog, but also because it's laid back, with good food, good company and good staff. Will definitely be returning soon. I fancy a go on one of their roast dinners.

✎ *pompeylass, March 2004*

The Nelson

Wood Green
232–234, High Road, London N22 8HH
☎ 020 8889 1697

The Nelson is the best pub in the world (well, in Wood Green). It's lively, there's lots of young people, good atmosphere and bar people are friendly. There's pool, karaoke and a dance floor – what more could you want in life?

✎ *s2thafizzle, December 2005*

Reasonable pub if you get in early. Comfortable, if unspectacular, environment. Decent bar service and a reasonable range of well-looked-after drinks. Price is pretty average. Has one of those Internet jukeboxes so you can get a variety of music played at certain times, but there is a tendency to show R'n'B-flavoured music channels on the TV and play the sound throughout the pub in the evenings.

Have seen trouble in here, but only rarely in fairness, and neither I nor my mates felt intimidated or in imminent danger of coming to any harm on any of these occasions. Has a late licence, so always an option for a last couple of drinks on the way home, but be warned that for this reason it can get uncomfortably packed with drunken fools.

✎ *Mr.Monkfish, October 2005*

You could do a lot worse in Wood Green than end up in the Nelson. I've been using this establishment on and off for about 12 years. I remember the Rattle and Hum days when there used to be posters on the walls and the occasional live band playing, but I prefer it now. Great pub for watching live football on the big screen (can't be beaten when England are playing), and it has a karaoke and late licence for some nights. Busy young crowd from the area but never any trouble. I highly recommend the Nelson.

✎ *ganger, March 2005*

The Nobody Inn

Newington Green
92 Mildmay Park, London N1 4PR
☎ 020 7249 6430

Went again for quiz – just as good. Nice local – wish it was a teensy bit closer to my flat. There's a quiz on Sunday too. It's not cheap, it's but a good pub. Wish it was a bit bigger to make it even better.

✎ *ronnierosenthal, September 2005*

Did the quiz here on Thursday – really friendly atmosphere and a prize even though we got spanked! Nice-looking pub, and it seems to show a lot of live sport. Will be back again

✎ *ronnierosenthal, August 2005*

Very friendly pub and great staff. Offers something for everyone – you can lounge on the sofas at the front, or there's a more traditional pub feel at the back, with pool tables and sky sports.

✎ *Anonymous, August 2005*

A great local in the heart of Newington Green. Good place to meet, showing all live sport.

✎ *Anonymous, April 2005*

The Oakdale Arms

Harringay
283 Hermitage Road, London N4 1NP
☎ 020 8800 2013

A real pint of mild in London. I have searched high and low for mild in London – here my thirst was quenched. Popped in as I only live around the corner. Several real ales are on tap. For me, it is the Milton Minotaur Mild.

Directions are easy, but about 15 minutes from Manor House Tube. Out of Tube, walk down the hill (Green Lanes) and turn right at the lights, down Hermitage Road. Eight minutes down there to an oasis of real ale.

✎ *pint_o_mild_please, January 2006*

Tried this place out on the strength of the reviews on this site and am pleased to report that they are accurate and I wasn't disappointed. To say this pub is a little off the beaten track might be an understatement, but persist in seeking it out and you'll find a positive temple to beer in an area that, the Salisbury on Green Lanes aside, is crying out for decent boozers. This pub must not be allowed to close!

From the outside, this pub looks like a bog-standard local pub. Once inside, your heart may initially sink as the decor owes more to a 1970s' working men's club than to a cosy traditional pub or a modern, clean and interior-designed chain pub. But settle in and it's comfy enough, if a little lived-in.

Now to the reason for the existence of this place: the beer. In a word, it's fantastic. Well-kept and reasonably priced real ales that you won't find anywhere else locally that taste absolutely gorgeous. I had pints of Jericho, which sadly ran out or I'd have sunk a fair few of them, but my alternative choice, Aphrodite, was also splendid and prevented my initial sadness at the end of the Jericho from ruining my evening.

Not much for lager drinkers (which normally includes me) except Budvar, but in fairness that's a fine beer in its own right and there are plenty of other places to go if you want to drink lager.

Well worthy of a visit. I shall be calling again.
✎ *Mr.Monkfish, December 2005*

Q. Where do you ever see the first pint of the session being pulled to clear the pipes?

A. Virtually nowhere, except here.

Q.   Where do you ever see bar staff examining glasses for stains from the washer and then deciding to do an extra rinse to guarantee that they are just right?

A.   Virtually nowhere, except here.

The staff also ask whether you enjoyed your pint and the beer is top quality – what a great pub. Lucky locals. Everybody else – put yourself out and make the trip. There is even a happy hour.
✎ *mally, March 2005*

Terrific beer and friendly service make this a mandatory destination for anyone with a preference for real ale. A great addition for London.
✎ *SteveinLondonFebruary 2004*

The Prince of Wales Ale House

Highgate
53 Highgate High Street, London N6 5JX
☎ 020 8340 0445

I love this pub. Good Thai food, a tricky quiz and fairy lights!
✎ *dawnage, May 2005*

This is a great little pub – the best in Highgate since the Flask's fall from grace. It has decent beers, an attractive interior, friendly bar staff and a pleasant terrace/beer garden looking on to Pond Square. The Tuesday-night quiz is bloody difficult, but at least they don't ask you about characters in Coronation Street.
✎ *Gerontay, December 2004*

The Railway

Finsbury Park
Wells Terrace, London N4 3JU

Fine little pub. Quiet, unpretentious, efficient – all the things you want in a good pub.
✎ *keep_it_green, January 2006*

Great little place. Tucked away. Totally unpretentious, with efficient, unobtrusive service. It does actually remind me of pubs in Ireland, which is a bit of a rare thing.
✎ *dawnage, May 2005*

The Ranelagh

Bounds Green
82 Bounds Green Road, London N11 2EU
☎ 020 8361 4238

Sssshhhhh ... stop telling everybody about it! I didn't know the pub pre-improvements. It's my new local and costs a bit more than most, but it's worthwhile as it attracts the right age group/mentality, which makes it 'grown-up', and at last Wood Green pubs no longer exist for me (does a back-flip). One thing, though – I tried the BBQ – it is a wee bit pricey – a fiver for, well, not very much really – that's the only disappointment :o(Drop the price of this, guys, and you'll be perfect. No chance of a music licence I suppose (dreams on)?
✎ *elllie, September 2005*

The last time I was in the Ranelagh was just before the refurbishment and it was a bit of an old locals' boozer, not particularly bad but not good also. But now it's the proverbial dogs bollo7ks! The beer garden is multi-levelled, with ample seating, and the interior is contemporary. Didn't try the food menu because we weren't hungry, but judging by everyone else's plates the food looked great. They serve a wide range of Belgian beers (just try the cherry beer and forget the rest!), and you can smoke nearly anywhere, which will be unpopular with the non-smokers. The only minor whinge that I can think of is that the day of my visit (Sunday) the German(?) bartender's English was just passable and he nearly overcharged us by double for the round we purchased, but that was just a honest mistake. All in all, another great pub that improves the area by leaps and bounds.

✎ *ganger, June 2005*

Great new beer garden. A cool place to spend a lazy summer Sunday afternoon maybe. Covered area outside, so you can enjoy the outside even if it isn't the best weather. Excellent food and good service. Friendly bar staff – a great improvement on what this place used to be. Hope it succeeds, as there's nothing like this in the area.

✎ *Anonymous, June 2005*

The Rose and Crown

Stoke Newington

199 Stoke Newington Church Street, London N16 9ES

☎ 020 7254 7497

Great traditional pub. Cosy, friendly and good quiz nights.

✎ *Anonymous, March 2005*

Trad pub, Adnams on tap, Truman/Hanbury panelled interior, locals and couscous guzzlers side by side.
✎ *danrkelly, May 2004*

The Salisbury

Harringay
1 Grand Parade, London N4 1JX
☎ 020 8800 9617

Very, very, very nice pub. We headed in on a cold night after a long, long day and received a warm welcome in this warm comfortable environment. The pub itself could easily veer towards the ostentatious, on account of the impressive ironwork over the door and roomy wooden rooms. But friendly staff (made all the more obvious by how many regulars they knew the names and regular drinks of) certainly produce an excellent pub.

Food was very good (it can be hard to find good mussels in London pubs).

Good point about the chill, though: it's pretty spacious so it really doesn't heat up at all.
✎ *Billy_and_Me, November 2005*

Grandiose looking but not at all stuck-up boozer in an area where good pubs are thin on the ground. Excellent spacious interior with nice tiled floor, stylish big windows and a huge bar. Plenty of seats if you are prepared to scout around in the nooks and crannies for them. Range of beers is inspiring and well kept. Bar staff are unfailingly friendly but can be a little bit too relaxed. Only downside is that it's a little steep for this neck of the woods in the way that Mount Everest is a little steep. All in all, though, a fantastic pub worthy of making the trip to Green Lanes for. Wrap up warm if you are going here in the winter, as it gets very chilly.

✎ *Mr.Monkfish, October 2005*

Brilliant pub. Can't recommend it highly enough. Don't visit that often but I'm proud to call it my local. Fantastic Victorian architecture, top grub, a good range of proper bitters and Czech lager – and it attracts a good mixed civilised crowd. An amazing turnaround from the hovel that it used be a few years ago, when you used to go in and worry if you'd still have your teeth in your mouth by the time you left.

✎ *DrewSavage, June 2005*

Nice pub. Always somewhere to sit, even when it's busy. Pleasant, relaxed atmosphere.

✎ *beermann, January 2005*

This pub is on the 'historic pub interiors' section of the CAMRA website and it is easy to see why as soon as you enter the place. There are three separate areas around a large central ornate bar: a bright and airy bar that fronts on to the main road; a nice wooden floored area, which seems the most popular; and a quieter, more intimate area, with a wonderful mosaic floor. If that wasn't enough, there is also a comfortably furnished lounge at the back. Ridley's Old Bob and IPA were on, plus London Pride and Czech beer Litovel. The pub has a nice friendly laidback feel to it and deserves a visit, if only for the decor.

✎ *Millay, July 2003*

The St. John's Tavern

Archway
91 Junction Road, London N19 5QU
☎ 020 7272 1587

The pub at the front is OK but nothing special. However, the dining room at the back is one of my favourite places to eat in London. Great food and the staff seem a lot friendlier than the bar staff. It can get very busy and a bit noisy, but I've never had a bad meal or a bad night here. It's best to go in winter when you can really appreciate how cosy it is.
✎ *DaveTheDog, July 2005*

Best pub in Archway by a mile.
✎ *Anonymous, June 2004*

I just had an excellent half-pint of Deuchars IPA this afternoon. This is easily the best pub in the Archway area. It's a spacious gastropub with three ales on hand pump, and an extensive wine selection. I have not yet tried the food, but the menu looked very exciting. Soft Latin-style background music on minidisc during my visit, but large number of discs near the deck suggested a broad range of musical styles played. Definitely worth a visit.
✎ *ladnewton, July 2003*

The Swimmer at The Grafton Arms

Holloway
12 Eburne Road, London N7 6AR
☎ 020 7281 4632

Fantastic pub, great jukebox, away from the main road and therefore away from the chavs. A+

✎ *Anonymous, March 2005*

The Ridley's IPA was off yesterday, but the guy changed it for me and my friend. Shame the poor guy was on his own and you had to wait up to 15 minutes to be served. The Czech lager was good though.

✎ *ladnewton, July 2003*

I have visited the pub twice now, and had a good pint of Ridley's IPA (note they have the whole range plus Fuller's London Pride) on both visits. The food is excellent and cooked in an open kitchen to the right of the bar area. Staff quite friendly. I went there last week on the way back from Finsbury Park on the evening Arsenal were playing Manchester United and, although I am an Arsenal supporter, it was nice to have a football-free pub in the area. Do visit and give it a try.

✎ *ladnewton, April 2003*

The Taps

Enfield

29 Silver Street, Enfield, Middlesex EN1 3EF

☎ 020 8366 3377

Went to the Taps for the first time last Saturday and it was great! Loads of space but retained intimate feel as the pub opens up to the back, where there's plenty more room and cosy fireplace. Also big TV screens for watching sports. Came back for the advertised quiz on Tuesday night, which was just a £1 to enter, with the prize being a tab behind the bar – sadly didn't win but was a good laugh. Definitely going to make this a regular haunt. Clean, friendly and intimate. Perfect.

✎ *eric1, January 2006*

Definitely the best pub in the Enfield town centre area. A pleasant surprise located on the site of a long-defunct trendy wine bar. A rare modern pub that seems to have a little bit of character to it. Vaguely Irish theme running throughout, but not in the usual style of O'Neill's et al. Service is friendly enough and reasonably quick. Prices are neither great nor dire, but the beer is good. At its best on a weekend afternoon or straight after work, when the narrow gangway leading from the bar (on the left hand side immediately as you enter) to the back of the pub isn't congested with human traffic, and as such drinks can be procured quickly and easily and ferried to your seat without undue spillage. Nice flat-screen TVs for sport, and clean toilets! Wooden benches are surprisingly comfortable. A good effort all round and worthy of investigation.

✎ *Mr.Monkfish, May 2005*

The Twelve Pins

Finsbury Park
263 Seven Sisters Road, London N4 2DE
☎ 020 8809 0192

My favourite pub anywhere. Started going there for the footie, but now quite happy to go there even if just passing through the area. Best bar staff I've encountered. Always very, very quick, even when rammed with footie supporters. Good value quality food as well.

I've had some bloody good times over the years in this pub.
✎ *PMH273, January 2006*

Comfortable, friendly, not overpriced and completely unpretentious – it's a boozer (a proper Irish one with good Guinness and cheap food) – nothing more or less.
✎ *pablos13, November 2005*

Great for watching the football, always packed, great service. Prices are reasonable – thank God the place hasn't become like an All Bar One. Massive Irish contingency. Friendly boozer.
✎ *cider_murray, July 2005*

The Wellington

Kingsland
119 Balls Pond Road, London N1 4BL

Relaxed atmosphere, great music, and a delightfully mixed crowd of very lovely people (+1 adorable white cat).

Setting is clean and comfortable, with cosy tables and big leather sofas. A diamond in the very rough Balls Pond Road.
✎ *spacekadet, January 2005*

Nice original features, leather chairs and real ales alongside premium lagers.

Broadsheets available. Nice spot.
✎ *danrkelly, May 2004*

The Wenlock Arms

Wenlock
26 Wenlock Road, London N1 7TA
☎ 020 7608 3406

The last stop on our Regent's Canal pub crawl from Limehouse to Wenlock. The pub was packed with people and we had to stand outside in surroundings that are not the best.

But, of course, this is among the best pubs in London for real ales. I will try to come earlier next time.
✎ *rune, November 2005*

Great pub. Great beers. Fantastic atmosphere. I highly recommend going on a Friday night when the trad jazz band plays. One of the best pubs in London. Not to be missed.
✎ *alexdelarge, September 2005*

Initial reaction to my midweek mid-afternoon visit is that this is a gem, a really great find. Hidden among a housing estate and building site, you would normally find a rundown pub with a selection of crap lagers, but the Wenlock is different. They have six different real ales, a cider, a Trappist lager and a quality lager.

Although it has to be said that not a lot has been spent on decoration, this adds to its charm. On my visit, there was a friendly bunch of locals and I considered it quite crowded for the strange timeslot of my visit. Go and support this real-ale, live-jazz/blues, friendly pub.
✎ *graley, June 2005*

Fantastic pub with super range of real ales on tap. Went to a CAMRA fest there last weekend as part of a two-day pub crawl. Met some great folks in the upstairs hall serving Yorkshire brews. The two pints in the main pub were also wonderful. Great lively local crowd. Beatles playing softly in the background. Pickled eggs behind the bar. Amazing. Seek out this pub.

✎ *chipawayboy, November 2003*

This pub is like putting on favourite pair of shoes – warm and comfortable as soon as you're inside.

An absolute gem. And long may it and the staff remain. The salt-beef sandwedges (yes – wedges!) are legendary.

✎ *chippysupper, June 2003*

The White Hart

Stoke Newington
69 Stoke Newington High Street, London N16 8EL
☎ 020 7254 6626

Very good for football, especially the Arsenal games. The DJ can be a bit random – once they were playing loud techno at 4 p.m. on a Sunday afternoon as people were eating their lunch.

Interesting choice. The garden is good, though, as the only place round here with one this good is over at the Londesborough. It's very dark, so cosy for winter, but remains dark in summer, so head out the back to the garden.

✎ *robinson, January 2006*

Recently been enjoying the fantastic BBQ they hold every weekend in the enormous beer garden. Food great!

✎ *Anonymous, June 2005*

I only ever visit this pub to watch the football, but I can honestly say that it is a great place to go with a great bunch of people there. Being able to watch a midweek European fixture, drink beer and still be able to order bar food after work is one luxury I can't be without.

✎ *Pat72, November 2004*

North West

The Albert

Primrose Hill
11 Princess Road, London NW1 8JR
☎ 020 7722 1886

The garden is a great place to drink.

Found the food to be very good. Location near the park makes it a convenient place for a weekend lunch.
✎ *Mr.Matt, August 2005*

For five years this was my local pub and I loved it. Cosy and welcoming in the winter, delightful beer garden in the summer: sit under the apple tree for a game of apple Russian roulette – whose head will the next one fall on? Food quite nice but pretty expensive.
✎ *jossv, June 2005*

The Black Cap

Camden
Camden High Street, London NW1 7JY
☎ 020 7428 2721

I love this pub. Great beer, good cabaret (most of the time), good staff (most of the time). If you are in Camden and fancy a quick pint, give this superb gay venue a go. 10/10.
✎ *Mr.Raffles, November 2005*

Lovely beer terrace and nice bar with good drinks. Spoiled by a minority of snooty gay men making me and my friend feel very unwelcome. OK, we did stand out as being very straight, but hey – we just wanted a beer!
✎ *Anonymous, March 2005*

Camden's premier gay pub, featuring a cabaret and disco stage on the ground floor and a quieter upstairs bar. Open late. Roof-garden area, which is pleasant in the summer. Sadly, as with many pubs of this type, there is no cask-conditioned real ale. Shame, as I'd go there more often if it did. The only bitter (keg) is Worthington's. Quite good food at lunchtimes. The pub runs its own cab-licensing service to ensure a safe ride home late at night, which is a great idea if you feel vulnerable for any reason. Hope someone from the pub reads this!
✎ *Anonymous, April 2003*

The Black Lion

Kilburn
274 Kilburn High Road, London NW6 2BY
☎ 020 7624 1424

Gorgeous pub, but the crowd is a bit too trendy at weekends. Worth a look in at lunchtime – the food is cheap and very good.
✎ *SusanC, November 2005*

Pricey. Not too many seats available. A nice old boozer nonetheless. Clientele is a bit more upmarket (in Kilburn terms) because of increased prices. You get what you pay for, I suppose.

✎ *keep_it_green, July 2005*

Went here last night with my flatmate and was astonished at this oasis of calm in Kilburn – most other places look like local pikey mosh pits. Dark, moody ambience, lavish, over-the-top ceiling, and a young not-about-to-start-random-fights crowd. Absolutely lovely. Of course, they've had to price out the riffraff, so two pints of Standard Wasser came to over a fiver, and a small bowl of pistachios cost £1.75. Tschh!

First impressions were that the Black Lion seemed a lovely place to while away some time, but you'll be paying a premium to feel relaxed drinking in Kilburn – mind you, everywhere seems to be gentrifying too.

Where are the chavs drinking nowadays? A mystery.

✎ *Ruby, September 2004*

The Clifton Hotel

St. John's Wood
96 Clifton Hill, London NW8 0JT
☎ 020 7372 3427

Funny one, this. Tucked away down a plush leafy street, you get the impression that it is a bit a private members' club for the well-to-do residents. It's nice enough, though, and there's seats outside, but there's a lot of cricket-jumper-round-the-shoulders action, etc., so doesn't really feel like a boozer and thus ain't really my scene.

It's the type of place that, if it pushed itself, would be mobbed by the bussed-in types that frequent the places to be in areas like, say, Westbourne Park (sorry, Westbourne Green). Would love to see the faces on the regulars if, say, a mid-range Audi with Essex plates, full of Armani-wearing tools, pulled up on a Saturday evening, drum 'n' bass blaring, looking for this gaff as a pre-club venue. There would be a swift meeting of several committees in the week after that, I can tell ya!

✎ *kmcs, August 2005*

Delightful. Huge conservatory, good sofas, quiet and relaxing during the week.

✎ *amphalon, March 2004*

The Corrib Rest

Queens Park
76–80 Salusbury Road, London NW6 6PA
☎ 020 7625 9585

Amen to kmcs below. This is the best pub in the area by a mile, and the comments about the football are spot on. I have watched loads of games in here because I like the beer and the atmosphere, but it can get full of these new Queens Park types, the less said about which the better. Ignore them and enjoy the friendly staff and unique music on offer.

✎ *barnetblackdog, February 2006*

A good pub. One of the few decent, friendly Irish pubs left in this area. Beer is fine, prices are good and the people are sound.
✎ *keep_it_green, July 2005*

I probably use the Corrib about once every two months and often come away thinking that I really must come more often. There's loads wrong here, ridiculous staff uniforms, overcharging for hiring the function rooms, really bad bands booked at the weekend ... However, there is so much more right about it. The staff are generally very friendly, there is a very wide range of people in here, an excellent pool table, and it actually feels like somewhere you can relax and unwind, unlike any other pub on the Salusbury Road.

Agree strongly with the comments from kmcs below about the football here. I have seen people in here watching a game without a drink, and then the minute it is over going to the Salusbury to buy one. Unbelievable. Indeed, the pub scenes from Spaced were filmed in here.
✎ *JohnMcC, April 2005*

The way this pub empties out after sporting events is a damning indictment of the type of people that kick around in Queens Park these days. This is by far the best pub in the area. Wicked service, good atmosphere and spacious, and yet loads of people in the area seem to prefer standing room only and inordinate waiting times at the Salusbury – they're welcome to it. The Corrib is quality, good for Prem football on Saturday afternoons (on the moody Greek satellite as well). Unfortunately, dead in the evenings, as mentioned previously.
✎ *kmcs, April 2005*

Isn't this where Spaced was filmed? If so, I'm definitely visiting for a swift one!

✎ *yourhardkorehero, March 2005*

The Crown and Anchor

Euston
137 Drummond Street, London NW1 2HL
☎ 020 7255 9871

Nice ale, and not too expensive. Really enjoyed the smoking balcony!

✎ *mmmpktge, October 2005*

Decent meet-up/post-drink type of place for the curry houses. Dead, but pleasant enough on a Saturday too.

Beer cheap, food appetising and good value, no bouncers or loud music, very pretty and friendly bar staff, mainly office workers and no drunks or chavs, etc., so gets the thumbs-up 'ere.

✎ *darloexile, April 2005*

A nice bright pub with decent air-conditioning, making it an ideal retreat when there's trouble on the trains at Euston.

Large open frontage and outside seating in the summer. Efficient and friendly service.

✎ *Millay, August 2003*

The Devonshire Arms

Camden

33 Kentish Town Road, London NW1 8NL

☎ 020 7284 0562

People need to get over the whole dress-code thing. I went there on several occasions, usually in jeans, trainers and a band T-shirt that may have been 'alternative' but not Goth (i.e. The Smiths, AFI, The Misfits, Slayer, etc.). I figure my long hair and usually being with a genuine Goth or two helped, but the worst I ever got was a friendly 'I'm sorry, but you'll have to take that off to come in' when I was wearing my warm jacket that has Adidas-like stripes (but isn't Adidas) on it and when I did, I was allowed entry. I was also given a friendly 'Well, we'll admit you this year, but next time you'll have to do better' for my half-arsed costume on Halloween.

I don't think you can judge a whole pub on a bouncer's mood on one occasion (i.e. only one factor), The dress code seemed pretty loose to me.

Even though I'm not a Goth, I enjoyed the genuine Goth atmosphere and the music crossed genres a bit (I remember hearing Ministry and Razed in Black to go along with Bauhaus and Fields of the Nephilim). I also really enjoyed the late licence. I did feel very hesitant about going here with any non-Goth friends, but it's nice to have a (rare) place for Goths to not worry about being harassed (although people do seem much more open-minded in London than in the States, generally).

✎ *AnotherYankeePoof13, December 2005*

A fantastic Goth boozer. If only there were more of its kind. A breath of fresh air from chav filth, estate trash, and brain-dead football-watching drooling zombies. All hail the Dev!

✎ *Pertwee, October 2005*

A local pub for local Goths. A great pub, but as has been mentioned to death here (pun intended), you'll have trouble getting in unless you look the part or you're a regular. Definitely a must-see if you're of an alternative persuasion though. If you're not, you probably won't like it and probably won't get in.

✎ *DJ.Alexander, April 2005*

I've not been to this pub for a while but have always liked it. They won't serve me now because I don't meet their dress code. How ironic that the Goths have turned into establishment snobs. To any Goth who says they get badly treated elsewhere, I say two wrongs don't make a right. One day, we will have a tolerant world and places like this will not be able to discriminate against people because of how they dress.

✎ *tgould, October 2004*

The Duke of Hamilton

Hampstead
23 New End, London NW3 1JD
☎ 020 7794 0258

This is a real gem. Was in there Xmas Eve and can't think of a better pub to spend it. Perched at the bar, a bit of banter with the genial landlord and plenty of well-kept ale. Not one to go to in a group,

though – enjoy it quietly with a few friends to really appreciate it.
✎ *OldRogue, January 2006*

Excellent Fuller's beers – best London Pride for miles around. Nice rolls at lunch time. Good mixture of locals, from the trendy to the professional to the unemployable.

A serious pub for serious boozers. Some great sporting pictures on the walls – landlord (Woody) is very keen on his rugby and cricket. Theatre next door adds to the people mixture. Nice outside terrace with well-maintained plants – good spot to while away time with a pint.
✎ *D.Bookless, April 2005*

An immaculately maintained Fuller's pub. The beer quality was top rate and the landlord served the best pint of 1845 I've ever had. Well done.
✎ *Dr_J, November 2003*

Noting that the Duke of Hamilton had recently been awarded the CAMRA North London Pub of the Year award, I set out to pay it a visit. Initially I was disappointed as it had a bit of a tourist trap feel to it, but it grew on me the longer I was there. The ESB was spot on and large single malts were selling for £3.30.

There is a reasonable range of beers, especially bottled, with friendly and (mostly) knowledgeable staff. It is well located on a quiet side street off Heath Street, and the raised seating area outside makes the pub very welcoming. A good choice, CAMRA!
✎ *Millay, August 2003*

The Euston Flyer

Euston

83 Euston Road, London NW1 2QU

☎ 020 7383 0856

Have been to this pub on many occasions when travelling out of Euston. My liking for this pub has reached the point now where I actually turn up an hour before my train to give me time for a couple of pints. An oasis in a commuter desert.

✎ *Beermeup, October 2005*

Cannot better the other descriptions given. Just to say that I have used the Flyer several times as a rendezvous when meeting up in the King's Cross area and never had a bad pint of Pride or ESB. One of our crowd (who will be nameless – you know who you are, Tony) drinks the Chiswick, but we do not like to talk about him.

✎ *Gann, October 2005*

Anyone who has made the unfortunate mistake of walking into the shambles that is Euston's O'Neill's will appreciate the Flyer just for being 30 yards down the road. However, besides the plus point of simply existing, the Flyer has a nice (if slightly touristy) atmosphere and a decent drink selection and is very spacious and well maintained for a pub that is basically aiming to catch commuters. It also has nice and plentiful window seats overlooking Euston Road – OK, this wouldn't, despite the enticing description, make my 'top ten views from pub windows' chart, but there is something strangely soothing about sipping a pint quietly while watching London speed past at its usual heart-attack-inducing pace.

It's not, therefore, the greatest pub on the planet, but for its location and what it sets out to achieve it's a decent enough watering hole. 7/10.

✎ *pgazz, April 2005*

The Flask

Hampstead
14 Flask Walk, London NW3 1HG
☎ 020 7435 4580

Fine pub – still the best bet in Hampstead. Every time I go here, I keep expecting Young's to have vandalised the pub and knocked it through into one bar. Thankfully, they haven't done so yet. The conservatory-type restaurant at the back seemed popular.

✎ *JohnBonser, April 2005*

A very old-fashioned pub, with its two parts split into the lounge and public bar. Full of people whose livers have seen better days – always the sign of a good pub. A proper old pub – not many around these days.

✎ *TheGP, February 2005*

This place was a real find. Tucked away down a charming side street right by Hampstead Tube, it has a perfect location. It is a really nice-looking pub and well laid out, with plenty of bar space and a nice conservatory for food out back. A good range of Young's beers, including Waggle Dance, one of my favourite thirst quenchers on a summer's day. Didn't stay long but I'm sure I'll visit again.

✎ *Millay, August 2003*

The Gate Lodge

Golders Green
622 Finchley Road, London NW11 7RR
☎ 020 8458 6258

I often pop into this pub after a few in the Refectory. A good pub to
have a few quiet pints and a chat with friends. A bit on the smoky
side sometimes though.
✎ *lennie384, July 2004*

I've got something of a soft spot for this pub. Located right next to
a busy road, it's besieged from the outside by people queuing for
any one of the hundreds of buses that seem to stop there.
Once you've fought your way in, however, you'll be pleased to find
a warm, cosy establishment where it's not unusual to find punters
playing chess on a weekday evening. There's a couple of TVs for
the football, but it doesn't dominate the pub and drown out the
conversation at all.

You're not going to have the best night of your life here, by any extent.
But it's the kind of place where you might happily sit back, neck a cou-
ple of slow pints and resolve to do something more exciting next week.
✎ *Slipperduke, February 2004*

The Good Mixer

Camden
30 Inverness Street, London NW1 7HJ
☎ 020 7916 6176

Basic and unpretentious and something of a local legend. Usually a lively and cosmopolitan (but ultimately friendly) mixture of punters. No matter how busy it is, you always seem to get served immediately. Great jukebox. Just possibly the best pub in Camden.
✎ tim_eyles, November 2005

Forget the whole Britpop thing and just enjoy a good old-fashioned unpretentious pub. Inexpensive, good atmosphere, a lovely lived-in charm and a decent jukebox.
✎ Mr.Monkfish, September 2005

My brother knows a bloke who sold his dad's car coat to Graham Coxon in the Mixer years ago. The place is steeped in Britcrock. The question when drinking in here tends to be 'Why?' The answer is that it's a decent little pub for a pint before making one's way to the latest disappointing Fall gig.
✎ tpk1, September 2004

The Hawley Arms

Camden
2 Castlehaven Road, London NW1 8QU
☎ 020 7428 5979

I love dropping into this pub on a Friday night – there's always a good crowd, and they always have the funkiest music.

I don't think I've been in yet and left without hearing Curtis Mayfield or James Brown.
✎ mrfrisky, August 2005

Beer in the Evening

I've drunk (and been drunk!) in nearly every pub in the Camden Town/Chalk Farm area. Accept no substitute: this is the best boozer in the area. Not only is there a good selection of beers (bottled and draught, kept-well and at prices reasonable for Camden), but also there is an awesome array of whiskies and other splendid spirits, served by the friendliest and most likeable staff I've ever met in London (and you can't put a value on things like that when you're a regular liquid luncher). By day, it's a nicely lit, spacious place to lunch and relax; by evening, it has a lively but warm atmosphere and there's nice seating for tastes both comfy and hard, a tasteful and eclectic jukebox and – beyond all doubt – the best pub grub in town, with items ranging from the classic (a beautiful steak/ale pie and mash, beer-battered fish and chips with mushy peas) to the whimsical but welcome (egg and soldiers – inspired!) – and all cooked from scratch to order.

It would almost be a shame to rate this pub highly and raise its profile: after all, you wouldn't want just anyone in on your secret, would you?
✎ *Paulie, February 2005*

Drinking in Camden can be a chore (something I'm not often known to say when booze is involved), what with surly regulars, moody staff and dubious jukeboxes. The Hawley, however, since the new management has taken over, has become something of an oasis. The staff make nipping in for a pint a pleasure, and an evening session feels more akin to chilling in a mate's living room than visiting a public house. With an excellent menu, a cracking jukebox – with a little of something for everybody – and a decent selection of drinks, this really has become the place to go for a night, or indeed a lunchtime, out. Slaínté!
✎ *danny_cascarino, February 2005*

The Head of Steam (Doric Arch)

Euston
1 Eversholt Street, Euston, London NW1 1DN
☎ 020 7388 2221

No fewer than ten real ales available here, and those that I managed to sample were all well kept. The place has a pleasant atmosphere, but you have to compete with football on the TV and memorise the access code for the loos, which latter task becomes perversely increasingly difficult to achieve as you work your way through the real ales and the need to bring it to mind becomes more and more frequent.
✎ *Raimundo, November 2005*

Do you sport a beard? Are you a member of CAMRA? Yes, this is the place for you. A marvellous selection of real ales, and a roaring fire too. This is the place for those cold winter afternoons. Situated in a tower block next to Euston Station.
✎ *tanderson7, October 2005*

Did return on Saturday and I can see no major changes. Two Fuller's beers and all usual guests available. Only thing I did notice was two tables had gone from the non-smoking area. I can live with that.
✎ *M. Sticker, August 2005*

Fears confirmed. Shut Monday and Tuesday next week for 'Fullerisation' of cash systems and suchlike. Apparently three Fuller's beers to be stocked and six guests. Wait and see.
✎ *mally, July 2005*

Rumour of sale to Fuller's very soon. Hopefully just a rumour. If I want Fuller's, there are plenty of places where it can be found. However, this place is almost unique in central London for beer quality and variety. Does anybody know more about the sale?
✎ *mally, July 2005*

Great to see a pub in London with such a wide range of real ales. Well worth popping into if you're in the area.
✎ *Darren_in_the_City, September 2003*

The Holly Bush

Hampstead
22 Holly Mount, London NW3 6SG
☎ 020 7435 2892

I thought this place was great. Really good selection of beers, historic interior, lovely location. Very quiet mid-afternoon on a weekday when I visited – just an old boy dying in the corner and a few other punters.
✎ *Stonch, January 2006*

I love this wee pub. It's out of the way. A proper secret boozer. Great little nooks and crannies. Its an old-school pub. Very pleasant.
✎ *dgriffin, September 2005*

Splendid pub – well worth visiting. Note the exceptional Benskin's mirror in the front bar. Admire also the old glasswork. Note for prospective customers: avoid Sunday lunchtime, when virtually the whole pub is laid out for diners and there is nowhere to sit. Note also that the local council prohibits drinking outside on the pavement, so there isn't this option for avoiding the crush.

✎ *JohnBonser, April 2005*

Well-hidden place, but unexpectedly massive inside. Absolutely packed as well. What looks like a quiet, old man's pub from the outside. A decent pub.

✎ *TheGP, February 2005*

I love this pub. I love it like a very fluffy puppy that's so soft and adorable that I could just stare at it all day. It's warm, it's sweet, it's got good beer, nice staff, good lighting, and it's in a decent neighbourhood. In short, there is nothing bad about this pub. It's brilliant. Top of the list. King of the hill. Pick of the pops. Up there! Up where? Up there, my friend. At the top. Yes. Very much so.

✎ *Slipperduke, October 2004*

Kingsfield Arms

Harrow
111 Bessborough Road, Harrow, Middlesex HA1 3DF
☎ 020 8422 2727

Very welcoming landlord and friendly, efficient staff. Real ale and selection of wines by the glass. Quiz each Tuesday – very popular. Attractive flowering baskets outside and very pleasant small beer garden at the back. It's a good place to relax after a hard day. The only trouble is that we enjoy it so much we can't keep away from the place.

✎ *SILVERARROW, September 2005*

A great spot for a summer's afternoon, with windows on to two streets and a merry little beer garden at the back. Draught IPA is in prime condition.

✎ *mikem, August 2003*

The Lord Palmerston

Dartmouth Park
33 Dartmouth Park Hill, London NW5 1HU
☎ 020 7485 1578

One of my favourites. Usually go here for some food rather than just as a drinking pub. The steak is better than at all the other local gastropubs and apparently has always been a good lunchtime stop since back in the day. Somewhat agree about the punters, but although you do get some attitude from New Labour wannabe-Hampstead types, this is a little unfair as there is usually a differing range of punters in here. One of the local old boys brings his dog in for a beer, which is always a good sign of a relaxed pub in my book.

✎ *rebelde, May 2005*

An exceptional gastropub! Go for the daily-changing menu that is always impressively stacked with imaginative meat, fish and veg options. The wine list is good too, if a little European. Once you get a table, a good evening is more or less guaranteed. Don't go if you don't like the well-to-do North London New Labour type, as they are wall to wall.

✎ *pub_numpty, May 2004*

Ordnance Arms

St. John's Wood
29 Ordnance Hill, London NW8 6PS
☎ 020 7722 0278

A nice find, a Sam Smith's pub in such a posh area. As such, it is a bit more fancy than your usual Sam Smith's pub.

Not much atmosphere, but a decent pub all the same.
✎ *TheGP, September 2005*

Not bad at all – a good Sam Smith's pub.
✎ *amphalon, March 2004*

Nice place, good atmosphere. Not much of a wine selection, but good food.
✎ *amphalon, November 2003*

The Pineapple

Kentish Town
51 Leverton Street, London NW5 2NX
☎ 020 7284 4631

A very good little pub; food excellent, especially the summertime barbeque. Some members of staff quicker than others, but that's to be expected I guess. All in all, a good place to waste an evening.
✎ *Anonymous, September 2005*

Visited this pub on 28 December 2004 on the recommendation of a friend of a friend. Fantastic. Super-cosy, great interior, great beer (Adnams, Pedigree, Pride) and nice loos (don't get that over in Hackney). I would be a regular if I lived locally but I don't, so ... bugger!

✎ *danrkelly, December 2004*

Nice pub, hidden away from the masses, even on busy nights with gigs at the Forum. Friendly staff, good old-fashioned atmosphere, and the food was great.

✎ *Claret_and_blue, December 2004*

One of very few pubs in London that keep a good pint of Marston's Pedigree. It's worth a visit, even if just on that count. Friendly staff and a convivial atmosphere. Medium-level background music allows conversation at a comfortable pitch. A great example of a pub being rescued from oblivion – everyone's efforts in doing so were worth it.

✎ *ladnewton, March 2003*

The Princess of Wales

Primrose Hill
22 Chalcot Road, London NW1 8LL
☎ 020 7722 0354

The best pub in the area by far. Brazilian boys behind the bar very friendly and show the meaning of quality service. Food excellent and good value. Nice clientele. Always three ales on – generally Adnams, London Pride and one guest: *Good Beer Guide* regular.

Forget the poncey media bars near by (there isn't a mullet in sight within the Princess – well, not in a retro sense). Come in, get warm by the fire, put your feet up, and drift off with a decent pint.
✎ *darloexile, December 2005*

The only authentic pub in Primrose Hill. Fantastic food, good beer, live jazz and interesting company. Highly recommended.
✎ *gjs34, October 2005*

Quinn's

Camden
65 Kentish Town Road, London NW1 8NY
☎ 020 7267 8240

One of my favourite pubs, and worth making a special journey for. They stock the largest range of German beers in London: usually about 20 of them, including Hefeweizen, Munich Helles Bier (pale lagers) and Dunkel (dark lagers). They're almost all sourced from Bavaria, except for the occasional Kölsch, and the range constantly varies but always includes interesting beers that you won't find anywhere else in London. There's usually something I've never tried before. Added to this, there's an even bigger range of Belgian beers and three cask ales on the pumps (Greene King IPA and a couple of others). It attracts a varied, unpretentious crowd.

I've never been unable to find a seat. There's a beer garden at the back for warmer weather, and the pub has a quirky look that somehow makes me think of bars in Brussels. Superb!
✎ *red, December 2005*

Beer in the Evening

If you like your speciality beers, this is the place to go. A bit on the quiet side, but the fridge at the end of the bar stocks some of the greatest imported beers I've ever sampled. The more senior bar staff really know their stuff when it comes to these beers and will gladly help when it comes to choosing. My personal recommendation is the Trois Pistoles, a really dark fruity beer or the version of Guinness brewed by a Belgian company in Dublin to the original recipe. Strange but true.
✎ *Sm1, December 2005*

I love this place. So many foreign beers to pick. Yes, they are a bit expensive, but compared with other places (e.g. the Porterhouse and other random pubs) the prices are reasonable. Well friendly too.
✎ *Medicrob1, September 2005*

Environment: nice. Clientele: varied. Beers: myriad of wonderful brews. Price: ouch!
✎ *Mr.Monkfish, September 2005*

The Sir Richard Steele

Belsize Park
97 Haverstock Hill, London NW3 4RL
☎ 020 7483 1261

A really quirky pub. Well worth a visit just to see the incredible interior. Plenty has already been said about the toilets.

Always good fun, especially when the regulars are on a bender.
✎ *gjs34, October 2005*

A great pub. One of the few remaining that hasn't suffered insipid modernisation. Great atmosphere, live music, superb food (Thai – try the thin-egg-noodle soup with chicken), decent selection of drinks (Magners!), genuinely friendly and interesting people, plenty of room, beer garden, open late, etc. The only downside is the toilets, which are certainly basic.

However, overall it's a belter of a pub and anyone who doesn't like this sort of pub undoubtedly likes the All Bar One chain and probably reads the Daily Mail.
✎ *Dylarolla, October 2005*

If loud music, Z-list celebs, iffy beer and toilets from the dark age are your thing, try out the old Steeles. One of the few pubs in the area that tries to maintain a proper drinkers' pub feel in an area of excessive up-one's-arsiness. And the decor is second to none. Recently they did out the upstairs with sofas and big tables – only downside is you have to go downstairs to get a beer.
✎ *darloexile, April 2005*

The Spread Eagle

Camden
141 Albert Street, London NW1 7NB
☎ 020 7267 1410

Not too chuffed with the makeover. It's taken some of the atmosphere from it, especially the bay window area looking on to Parkway. I preferred it slightly careworn. Beer still spot on though.
✎ *Shelders, January 2006*

Beer in the Evening

I am a Young's lover and had a great pint of Winter Warmer here. Seems to be a nice place attracting a mix of people. A good choice in this area. Lovely girl behind the bar – very friendly too.
✎ *Stonch, December 2005*

Best bet for a traditional-style pub in Camden. Good location, nice building and decent beer. Could be cheaper, but then again where couldn't?

Nice relaxed atmosphere where you can easily get chatting to other drinkers or keep quiet and not be hassled if you just fancy a pint in peace.
✎ *Mr.Monkfish, October 2005*

My favourite pub in Camden. Quiet and comfortable. I don't think it's as good as in the heady '90s, though, when the atmosphere was always terrific and it was run by the inimitable John and Doreen.
✎ *dawnage, May 2005*

One of the few pubs in the Camden area where you feel confident ordering cask beer. This is another good Young's pub, with their usual range of lagers and bitters. Also a full range of Young's bottled beers, including the wonderful Double Chocolate Stout.

Not that well laid out, but there is a nice bright seating area and the food is good.

Attentive and friendly staff. Only criticism is the Gents toilets (both of them), which could do with some attention.
✎ *Millay, September 2003*

The Volunteer

Baker Street

247 Baker Street, London NW1 6XE

☎ 020 7486 4090

Far better than it has any right to be given its fairly uninspiring location. It feels more like a suburban pub rather than a central London commuter pub by a Tube, and is better for it. It does get busy, but it remains surprisingly tourist-free in a big tourist area.

✎ *cardamom, September 2005*

Quite a revelation having drunk there in its previous incarnation. Lots of European beers and three real ales, with the delicious Wild Hare from the Bath Brewery on at the moment. Although expensive, it's very pleasant to drink in a bar that treats its beer with so much respect. Having seen all the microbrewery pump clips dotted around the bar, there's obviously been some great nights recently. This was number two on a five-bar pub crawl last night – we never moved on.

✎ *SteveinLondonAugust 2005*

This was surprisingly alright actually. Quite busy, but just enough room, nice and dark, good selection of beer and friendly bar staff. Er, for once I've got nothing to whinge about!

✎ *Slipperduke, October 2004*

West

The Brook Green Hotel

Hammersmith
170 Shepherd's Bush Road, London W6 7PB
☎ 020 7603 2516

The standard in this pub is very good. The bar staff are efficient and well polished, the beer is very well kept, and the food is pretty good. The reworking of the Victorian features scores well too – the decoration is refreshingly done. At times it can lack a bit of atmosphere, particularly at the southern end of the pub, but otherwise it deserves a lot of praise.
✎ *LovePubs, December 2005*

This is an excellent pub on Shepherd's Bush Road. Came here on a Wednesday night and it was not too packed. Food was delicious, and waiting staff were great in all senses of the word. A nice place to enjoy good beer and food.
✎ *slb, June 2005*

A splendid example of how a pub can be updated without being spoilt. Very impressively ornate bar with glasswork. High ceilings. Reasonably warm and welcoming atmosphere. Young's beer was on reasonable form. They are doing a BBQ for Australia Day – 26 January.
✎ *JohnBonser, January 2005*

Beer in the Evening

A really great pub with a good atmosphere and surroundings and a good set of regulars. I discovered this pub when I was looking for a decent pub when attending Fulham's games at Loftus Road.

I went there before and after every home game and never had a bad pint – or a bad experience. It is very much a rugby pub but that shouldn't stop other sports-lovers going there.

Unfortunately, Fulham has moved back to Craven Cottage so I have not been back since the end of last season. If I am in the area, I will be sure to drop in for a pint.
✎ *gearbox, October 2004*

The Carpenters Arms

Marble Arch
12 Seymour Place, London W1H 7NA
☎ 020 7723 1050

Excellent pub, and guest ales all on form. Customers friendly. Same group as the Market Porter – need I say more?
✎ *canastajim, October 2005*

A gem. Order yourself a pint of one of the many ales on sale, enjoy the atmosphere and relax. Also great for watching sport on Sky if that's your thing.
✎ *TonyAle, January 2005*

Went there on Friday night – I must admit the music was a little loud (but not so loud you couldn't hold a conversation.)

There was a great atmosphere, though – mainly because the bar staff seemed to be enjoying themselves so much (but they still served you quickly). Will definitely be back.
✎ *gilesd, July 2004*

Good beer range, and kept well. Very noisy though in my opinion, especially when the big ceiling-mounted TVs are all on.
✎ *mym, June 2004*

The Chancellors

Hammersmith
25 Crisp Road, London W6 9RL
☎ 020 8748 2600

Nice cheery pub, which makes a very pleasant change from the usual Hammersmith fodder. Great beer and a brilliant location all add up to one of the best boozers in west London. 10/10.
✎ *Mr.Raffles, November 2005*

Great find! A dream on a summer afternoon, particularly if you are visiting the Riverside Theatre across the road – at least half the price of Riverside beers.

Best quote: 'It's ancient, as are the locals, and the Lady behind the bar deserves the capital 'L' – she's great!'
✎ *mikem, August 2005*

Small pub in side street. Friendly enough. Famously opens at 10.30 in the morning, with sad old gits normally called Robin already queuing up waiting to buy their gin and tonics. Very pleasant in summer sitting outside the front of the pub in the sunshine by the Thames.

✎ *peterthebeetle, February 2005*

Nice little local pub. Bit Irish. One for the oldies. Good spot for an afternoon quiet pint.

✎ *TheGP, September 2004*

The Churchfield

Acton
Station Building, Churchfield Road, London W3 6BH
☎ 020 8992 7110

Prices have increased since my last review (August 2005) and happy hour is now just one hour, but this is still the best pub in the area for quality of food/drinks and service. Good selection of beers, including European bottled beers, such as Staropramen, Leffe and Artois Bock. Pub quiz on alternate Tuesdays, with cash and drinks as prizes.

Bar food is good quality, if a little expensive. House wine is drinkable and around £12 per bottle.

✎ *abacus3, January 2006*

I've just moved in down the road from the Churchfield, and it came recommended by my flatmates. Good selection of beers, reasonable prices (for London), music that's not too loud, and friendly staff. What more could you want from a local?

✎ *nonstick, November 2005*

A lovely quiet pub with good beers and interesting food. Lovely building, too, in the old railway station.

✎ *Anonymous, March 2004*

The Defector's Weld

Shepherd's Bush
170 Uxbridge Road, London W12 8AA
☎ 020 8749 0008

The DF is a considerable improvement over its previous incarnations (especially the awful Edwards) and has reintroduced real ales that are well kept, although the choice of Greene King IPA and Fuller's London Pride is a bit boring. Food was expensive but nicely done. When it is not full, it is a relaxing comfortable place if you like large lounge-like places and deserves recommendation for the Shepherd's Bush area.

✎ *LovePubs, December 2005*

This pub should be great. Looks good, sounds good and the drinks are super. Shame is that any evening of the week it's full. Not just full though, but full of idiots – another post calls them 'fashion victims all trying to vie for the most attention'. I heartily agree. My ideal night out is not walking in circles round this pub trying to find a seat being silently condescended by some twat leafing through his copy of Ariel. Either go during the day or go to the Goldhawk.

✎ *bumpby, October 2005*

Stumbled into this new tastefully refurbed pub in Shepherd's Bush. Amazing transformation from what it used to be like a few months

back. Great atmosphere, fast service and really friendly staff, who even had the time to explain what had been done. Then I went up to the new upstairs bar/dining area. Absolutely brilliant and food fantastic. Odd that such a place has appeared in grimey Bush, but with gaffs like this the future looks up. Well worth a visit or two.
✎ *Anonymous, December 2004*

The Dove Inn

Hammersmith
19 Upper Mall, London W6 9TA
☎ 020 8748 9474

My favourite pub so far along the Thames. Lovely warm and inviting pub. It is a bit on the tiny side, but it offers a fantastic real fire and that lovely Fuller's gem, Honey Dew. Lush! It has a nice olde worlde feel.
✎ *Tiny, January 2006*

Used to be very much my local when I lived in Hammersmith. Sunday nights in here and the Gorilla Round (TM) were legendary. I still like to pop in for a pint or two if I'm in the area. Would've rated a 10/10 when Martyn and Dianne were running it a few years back. A fantastic historic pub, riverside location to die for and gorgeous Fuller's ales.
✎ *tim_eyles, November 2005*

This is the best pub in Hammersmith. No competition. Any time of year, this shows all the other pubs how it should be done. I'd describe it more, but there's nothing more to say. Anything good about a pub is here.
✎ *triphere, July 2005*

Keep visiting this gem! I know I will. Great to see that London still has some decent pubs. Fuller's ESB sometimes varies, though. Try the Chiswick Ale – a great session bitter.

✎ *ladnewton, February 2003*

The Drayton

West Ealing
2 The Avenue, London W13 8PH
☎ 020 8997 1019

This is a great pub. Delicious, imaginative and reasonably priced food. Great downstairs disco and also accommodates chess and Rotaract clubs. The beer garden is amazing, with heated lamps for when it gets a bit chilly and a play area for children. The only downside is that there isn't much of an atmosphere and the staff can be quite rude.

✎ *bub, August 2005*

Great local pub. Fantastic-sized beer garden and good atmosphere. Only problem for 'outsiders' is that you'd have to get an overland train to West Ealing to appreciate its greatness.

✎ *lizziewill, December 2004*

Top pub and much improved since the refurbishments of a few months ago. Top food too, although it is a bit on the expensive side. Very lively in the evenings, good crowd, and none of the townies who blight town-centre pubs.

✎ *robbie2005, October 2004*

Would definitely echo all that has been said about this pub.

It's a top place, best beer garden I've seen, lively and atmospheric, good facilities (theatre, live music, big-screen TV for sport, pool table) – and the barmaids aren't bad either.
✎ *Chelsea_Loyal, October 2003*

Excellent! Went on the Weekly Wind-Up here on 3 July. Well-kept Chiswick. Lovely beer garden. The bar staff have a refreshing sense of humour, which is great to see.
✎ *ladnewton, July 2003*

The Fox

Hanwell
Green Lane, London W7 2PJ
☎ 020 8567 3912

Great pub. Nice locals. Tucked away down a side street.
✎ *silverside, January 2006*

This is what all pubs should be like – good beer, friendly peeps, nice garden, good food.
✎ *Boaby, January 2006*

Great selection of real ale and a must for a canal walker like me. They were having a beer festival when I called in. Super pub from the old breed. Check it out.
✎ *lordhicks, March 2005*

Seems to have become more food-oriented of late, particularly at Sunday lunchtime – most of the tables were reserved for diners last Sunday. Still, the Timmy Taylor was on top form and the pub is still an ideal stopping-off point when doing the Grand Union Canal, either on foot or bike (or barge). Pub is close to the famous Hanwell Locks.

✎ *JohnBonser, March 2005*

The Kings Head

Earl's Court
17 Hogarth Place, London SW5 0QT
☎ 020 7244 5931

Quality pub hidden away from the hubbub of Earl's Court. It's always busy, which can mean seats can sometimes be difficult to find, but it's worth persevering. The beer selection is very good and the food is excellent – I recommend the steak pie. One drawback is that although the waitresses are very sweet, their English can sometimes be almost non-existent, which means that ordering can sometimes be an interesting experience.

✎ *libero, February 2006*

The problem with most London pubs is that they have a tendency to be tribal. You know, folks going out in groups where everybody knows everybody else and it's difficult to break into a conversation and get to know new people. Not so with the Kings. There's a good cross-section, from tourists visiting the area to locals who could be anything from street-sweepers to city professionals. For most of the time you will find the locals friendly and welcoming. The staff are a cut above the usual, the choice of beers is good and reasonably priced for the area, and the selection of bourbon is damn hard to beat. The Kings is undoubtedly the best ale house in Earl's Court and probably the whole of K and C. See you in there!

✎ *Woolyback, December 2005*

Very nice pub. Different from the ones on the Earl's Court Road in that it's not full of weirdos. Can be tricky to get a seat as it's always busy, but this pub is definitely the best choice if you're drinking near the station.

✎ *libero, September 2005*

The North Star

Ealing
43 The Broadway, London W5 5JN
☎ 020 8579 0863

On a rare visit to this neck of the woods, I went in and was very happy with a great pint of Staropramen Granat. Seems to be a good selection of beers here. Clearly a pub for young people. Really liked it.

✎ *Stonch, January 2006*

It's a good pub, especially as the area surrounding it is filled with rubbish pubs/bars. Particularly like the interior in this place – old dark wood.

✎ *TheGP, February 2005*

Following on from my comment in November, I've just seen that the middle room is now a non-smoking area. Although it's not

completely separated from the other rooms, this is still good news. I shall rate it higher now!
✎ *lynshroom, January 2005*

I would rate it higher and go there a lot more if it would cater for non-smokers. It's got about three rooms, so why can't they have a non-smoking section somewhere?

I agree it's got a better atmosphere than most pubs around the area, but it's very smoky in my opinion, which makes me leave after one pint usually.

It's OK in the summer though, because there's a good outside space.
✎ *lynshroom, November 2004*

Excellent pub. Perhaps the best around the Ealing Broadway area. Decent music, nice atmosphere and some good beers.
✎ *jethro, October 2003*

The Old Pack Horse

Chiswick
434 Chiswick High Road, London W4 5TF
☎ 020 8994 2872

Lovely pub. Excellent Fuller's beers and so comfortable and lovely on a cold day. A real proper pub.
✎ *Alexh1982, January 2006*

What a change! Good beers, cosy place, especially when the fires are going, prompt service and friendly staff, plus a Thai restaurant. Speedy delivery of food and at a good price for the lunch crowd. Have found myself frequenting here more and more.
✎ *Flawed, December 2005*

Currently closed for refurbishment – reopening at midday on 5 October. Let's hope it hasn't been vandalised as it was a classic pre-closure.
✎ *JohnBonser, October 2005*

Good local pub with Thai food, run by the former manager of Latymer's on Hammersmith Road. Full range of Fuller's beers.
✎ *beeronaut, March 2004*

The Prince Edward

Bayswater
73 Prince's Square, London W2 4NY
☎ 020 7727 2221

Nice enough place – a bit worn but comfortable enough. A bit wide open for my tastes, with bar in the middle and big open room around it.
✎ *jorrocks, October 2005*

I have a perverse liking for this pub. It's a bit tatty round the edges but basically comfy, spacious and agreeable. Beer is usually good too. Not had any of the grub but it seems to do a good, reasonably priced spread. Good for a few pints before sampling the many

delights of the nearby 'street of a thousand restaurants' –
Westbourne Grove.
✎ *Ullage, May 2005*

Great back-street local-style pub. No loud music or TV,
friendly staff, excellent beer.
✎ *Graylob, April 2005*

The Queens Arms

South Kensington
30 Queen's Gate Mews, London SW7 5QL
☎ 020 7581 7741

Superb pub! Crowded on Friday but not unpleasant. Good beer in
cushy surroundings. And, of course, the car showroom opposite
is fun.

I also found the beer to be on tiptop form, and a good selection of
whisky was available as well.
✎ *Muzthing, December 2005*

Hidden in mews behind the Royal Albert Hall. Serves good real ale.
Quality of the food is good, although a bit pricey.

Enjoy as you contemplate which car from the garage across the
way you wish you could afford.
✎ *lout_from_the_lane, February 2004*

The Radnor Arms

Kensington
247 Warwick Road, London W14 8PX
☎ 020 7602 7708

Was in Kensington for a business trip and stumbled across the Radnor. The atmosphere was second to none. A real homely place, complete with a dog and cats and a fish tank. Unusual to find such a warm friendly place, but a real pleasure. Great beer and friendly staff. will be the first pub I go next time in town. What a fantastic place.
✎ *Davepearce, January 2006*

Nice locals' pub and good beer. Friday-night quiz quite popular. May be brought down soon, so get there quick and sign the petition to keep what is becoming a rarity in London, i.e. a traditional quality pub.
✎ *mrsjones, August 2005*

What a little gem of a boozer. The staff are lovely, the drink is excellent and the locals (I'm not one) are a lovely bunch. It seems this place may be under threat from the bulldozer, but this in my eyes would be a damn crime! Try this pub out – it's a real little find.
✎ *gizmo, August 2005*

Red Lion

Ealing
13 St Mary's Road, Ealing, London W5 5RA
☎ 020 8567 2541

Revisited this summer after a gap of many years (due to moving out of the area). As good as ever, and I can't think of any way of improving it, hence a rating of 10/10.
✎ *154e, September 2005*

Splendid pub as ever. A classic example of how a pub can be extended to broaden its appeal to a wider range of customers, without losing its local traditional feel. Look out for the photographs on the walls from old Ealing films, notably *The Ladykillers*.
✎ *JohnBonser, May 2005*

Went in here recently for the first time in 20-odd years. Apart from the extension, not a lot has changed. Oh, apart from the price of the beer. Still one or two faces I recognise from all those years ago – amazing that they are still alive, considering the amount of beer they consumed! Wonder if they've still got my tankard behind the bar?
✎ *wmon, April 2005*

Visited the pub on Thursday – had a great pint of Chiswick and the Summer Ale was good too. People in the pub seemed friendly, and there was a fairly convivial atmosphere. Note the pub appears to have been extended somewhat from its original tiny beginnings.
✎ *ladnewton, July 2003*

The Red Lion and Pineapple

Acton
281 High Street, London W3 9BP
☎ 020 8896 2248

Beer in the Evening

Typical Wetherspoon's pub – big, brash, cheap and cheerful. Beer and food are adequate and Sunday roast will fill you up until Tuesday. Low beer prices make up for slow service from the rare and endangered barmen. Lots of sportswear and mentals in here.
✎ *abacus3, January 2006*

The Wetherspoon's formula works here too. You know what you're getting and it's pretty good. Nice to get change out of a note when you buy drinks for three people. Staff are sometimes scarce and there are anguished looks on patrons' faces as they try to get served. Try taking a pretty daughter or handsome son to attract their attention. The under-age-admissions policy is a bit draconian. A 17-year-old would have to leave in the early evening. Pity, since there's a nice smokeless area that is ideal for eating.
✎ *pauldanon, November 2005*

The food here really is great. Also bought two double Jim Beams and coke and a pint and got change from a fiver.

The crowd are nice and friendly, only sometimes there needs to be more of an age balance rather than just the hardcore pensioners and the teenagers. Overall a good pub.
✎ *bub, September 2005*

A pleasant Wetherspoon's pub. I can imagine it gets very busy at the weekend. But I went for the curry night on Thursday and enjoyed it as it was fairly quiet. The food was good. It was cheap. Above all, I enjoyed leaving the pub (after sitting in the non-smoking area) not smelling of smoke.
✎ *Chantil, November 2004*

The Swan

South Acton

1 Evershed Walk, 119 Acton Lane, London W4 5HH
☎ 020 8994 8262

Wonderful pub – excellent food, superb wine list. Best in Chiswick.
Best in Acton.
✎ *lozatron, November 2005*

Once again, I must say what a fantastic pub the Swan is. The food
is absolutely fantastic and the service is great. It's also just been
voted one of London's top ten restaurants by Harden's – get in
quick before the crowds. Definitely my choice for Pub of the Year.
✎ *Anonymous, October 2003*

Recently refurbished as another Chiswick gastropub, but a very
superior one. The wine list looks fab, but I developed an instant
addiction to the Terre in Fiore the first time I went so I haven't got
much further with it! Food is great, staff are friendly, and there's
always a spare newspaper to read too. Shame they didn't do up the
loos when they did up the rest of it though.
✎ *oakleym, August 2003*

The Viaduct

Hanwell
221 Uxbridge Road, London W7 3TD
☎ 020 8567 1362

This pub has just had a makeover and is bright and airy, with good beer and food. They tell that on the last Thursday of the month the nurses from the hospital come down to spend their well-earned pay. One for the boys to look out for.

✎ *Boaby, January 2006*

I visited this pub the other day and it was fab – great selection of ales, which change every month. The refurb is fantastic – it really brightens up the place, which used to be a bit dull and dreary, and the locals are friendly. A definite asset to Hanwell, which has some dreadful pubs. Check it out, you will not regret it.

✎ *bub, October 2005*

Has now reopened. It has all been done quite nicely, without going over the top, so what you have is a nice pub with a more traditional standing bar at the East end and carpets and seating at the other. Even the toilets have been renovated! Wine list not bad, beers kept in good condition when we went in, and they seem to be trying some things with the food (fairly simple stuff but a weekly menu as well). Wish this place well – it deserves it!

✎ *jollid, April 2005*

The Victoria

Bayswater

10a Strathearn Place, London W2 2NH

☎ 020 7724 1191

This is a great little pub, and it retains its traditional interior. Friendly landlord and staff. Fuller's beer is always served in excellent condition. Main bar area is usually busy. There are function rooms upstairs and some seating outside. Popular quiz night on Tuesdays is good for a laugh.

✎ *fromedrinker, December 2005*

Lovely Victoriana type pub. If you are in the area, visit the theatre bar upstairs.

✎ *zagreb, January 2005*

Decent traditional pub.

✎ *nick.t, December 2003*

The Warrington Hotel

Maida Vale
93 Warrington Crescent, London W9 1EH
☎ 020 7286 2929

Good beer and great decor. Forget you're in London. Envious of locals (they must be minted to live round here).

✎ *redrocket, August 2005*

This place is jammed during matches, hopping on a warm day, and seemingly busy every day of the week. Warm, friendly, fun, great bar staff, and what an incredible architectural sight! Used to be a brothel owned by the Anglican Church. Order takeaway from Ben's and eat it outside on the picnic tables.

This place is for everyone, from whippersnappers to old fogies. Proper ales and guest beers served hand-pulled, and also all the

cold lagers the young guns love. If you are lucky and Penny is working, so much the better.
✎ *bossygirl, June 2005*

A very ornate and spectacularly good pub. If only it was nearer civilisation.
✎ *TheGP, March 2005*

The Wheatsheaf

Ealing
41 Haven Lane, London W5 2HZ
☎ 020 8997 5240

Nice pub. Planned on staying for one or two pints Friday night with a mate before moving on to the North Star, but found ourselves some seats – the Discovery was pretty tasty and somehow ended up staying for seven or eight. Bit smoky (yeah, I know – I did reek of smoke afterwards) but that's about the worst of it. I'll be going back for a few pints in the near future.
✎ *brodie_bruce, January 2006*

Excellent ales and staff.
✎ *bigbeerbelly, March 2005*

Nice locals' pub on a residential street that's far enough from The Broadway for you to forget that you're in Ealing. Good range of beers. Never tried the food, but looks pretty good.
✎ *burnsy, July 2004*

The Zetland Arms

South Kensington
2 Bute Street, London SW7 3EX
☎ 020 7589 3813

More and more I think this place is a good, good pub. Ale – great.
Decor – very good. Atmosphere – nice. Crowd – a surprising mix for
South Ken. They show the sport too. Good place.
✎ *Anonymous, December 2005*

Great pub, friendly, good service, great food. We managed to get a
table on a Thursday night and it was just quiet enough to have a
chat. Will be visiting again soon.
✎ *bonsai, December 2005*

Nice pub, nice mirrors, nice ale. Slow service but never had a bad
ale in there.
✎ *mitomighty, November 2005*

South West

The Abercorn Arms

Teddington
76 Church Road, Teddington, Middlesex TW11 8PY
☎ 020 8943 9484

Excellent pub. Good pool table and darts, friendly bar staff, cheap grub, really traditional. The place has character and seems to be very popular. Pints are a little pricey, but then again where are they not in Teddington?? It would be nice if it stayed open later as well. But yeh, a really nice pub. Definitely worth a visit.
✎ *full_english, January 2006*

The friendliest pub in the area, and yet to serve a dodgy pint to me. Mel, mine host, was former chef at the Press Club in London and the reputation of his food at the Abercorn is testimony to this. A cat-lover's paradise – punters are regularly treated to a visit from Alfie, one of the two pub cats – when he's not bolting for the cool of the cellar, that is. However, when Alfie's up to his mousing, the kitsch cats that adorn every windowsill are just as much fun, as are the caricatures of regulars drawn by an artistic regular. The lounge bar is a good retreat for the unsportingly minded on footie nights, although this is also a good outpost for rugby devotees from Twickers.
✎ *beerbaby, August 2005*

What a great little pub! Up Church Road, which is a long side street off Broad Street (the main drag, folks) and close enough to several other great pubs in order to make it a cert for any pub crawl you're planning. Kick off at the other Young's pub in Tedders, the Queen Dowager, then to the Mason's Arms, and then here for a taste of three really good pubs.

Two small-ish bars. It's a small managed house with the Young's usual ales in great condition. It's easy to imagine yourself as a regular here. It has a dead homely atmosphere, the place is spotless and the welcome is in evidence.

✎ *NewMaldenOrder, August 2005*

The Alexandra

Clapham
14 Clapham Common South Side, London SW4 7AA
☎ 020 7627 5102

As an earlier comment said, 'does exactly what it says on the tin'. Great for watching sport – went there for the Ireland v. Australia rugby a few weeks back and everyone had a great time and generally had good service. Watched a few other games there upstairs. Only big issue is that it gets really smoky – beyond the point of tolerable for some reason. Have to agree with another comment – have a mate and his wife who will only drink with me there. None of us can remember the end of our first night out there, and none more since. Strange, as we remember all the other nights out.

✎ *tour_contact, December 2005*

Decent boozer crammed full of your usual pub tat (old radios, tin signs, etc.). Handy for the Tube and serious drinking in the shadows.

✎ *redrocket, August 2005*

Great, great boozer. Gets packed for the big games, so get there early to bag a spot upstairs. Not full of freaks and posers, which is unusual for a pub near the Common.

✎ *TheClaw, July 2005*

The Alexandra

Wimbledon
33 Wimbledon Hill Road, London SW19 7NE
☎ 020 8947 7691

We visited the other day for lunch. The Young's bitter, house white and the fish and chips were all fine. Food portions were large and the cost wasn't too evil by London standards. Will go here again (I don't live south side no mo'). It's certainly my fave place to eat and drink in Wimbledon.

Staff were OK. It's pretty pointless to complain about staff in London pubs anyway, as they tend to last only a few weeks on average.

✎ *oak_cliff, December 2005*

Can't comment on the prices (not my round) but the quality of the bitter was excellent. A bit of a gloomy wood-panelled Young's pub, but conveniently located near the station.

✎ *lout_from_the_lane, August 2004*

Good pub with good beer. Big-screen TV for the sports. Good atmosphere. Nice roof terrace upstairs, which is perfect in the summer evenings to simply sit back and watch the world go by – I highly recommend it!

✎ *Lawrence_M, October 2003*

The Atlas

West Brompton

16 Seagrave Road, London SW6 1RX

☎ 020 7385 9129

Wonderful buzzy pub that's always full and serves amazing food. Service can be a bit brusque, but with the cosy inside and the nice little walled garden to the side, this is one of the best pubs in London.

✎ *libero, September 2005*

Although now a gastropub, none the worse for that.

Beers have always been drinkable. Retains the older-style wood-panelled interior of the pubs I learnt to drink in.

✎ *canastajim, July 2005*

Terrific busy little gastropub with a changing menu and interesting selection of wines and easily the best near West Brompton Tube. Caledonian IPA is consistently well kept, and you will always find something delicious to eat. It's closed over Christmas, so make it your New Year resolution to pay this great little pub a visit.

✎ *SteveinLondonDecember 2004*

Excellent. Local pub. Great atmosphere, if a little crowded at times. Food is to a very high standard. Music cool and at respectable volume.
✎ *yoooreds, September 2004*

Very nice. Good range of beers. Unspoilt interior. Some people have intimated they couldn't find it: on Old Brompton Road, find Earl's Court 2, by the Prince of Wales. Stand facing it and turn about through 180 degrees. You will be looking down Seagrave Road. The Atlas is down there on the left.
✎ *beeronaut, August 2004*

Baobab

Collier's Wood
222 High Street, London SW19 2BH
☎ 020 8540 3545

The food is pretty good here, and great BBQs in the summer. Shame the garden is on the main road. Cocktails are good. No real ales, but you can't have everything. Certainly one of Collier's Wood's two finest drinking establishments.
✎ *Flawed, December 2005*

The best pub in Collier's Wood (even after the Tup opened). Good beers, good cocktails, good food, nice atmosphere. The only drawback is that the beer garden is a bit smallish and on the main road. The staff are especially nice and really make a difference. I would recommend this place to anybody heading out this way.
✎ *Loki, September 2005*

With BBQ season kicking in, the temptation to chuck on your pinny and cremate a chook at home is often too much to resist for some. Thank god for Baobab! A huge terrace out the back and some of the best BBQ-ed food this side of the river make this place a must. When the sun goes down, slink indoors and relax in the bar, tapping your foot to a few grooves while enjoying a cold beer or fresh mojito from the thoughtful and yet unpretentious cocktail menu. And guess what? They even have clean fresh toilets for the ladies. All I can say is get involved.
✎ *yamin, June 2005*

Lovely little bar/pub with a very attractive menu. All service is friendly and they've got Pilsner Urquell on tap. Just what this area needs.
✎ *brionyot, November 2004*

Bread and Roses

Clapham
68 Clapham Manor Street, London SW4 6DZ
☎ 020 7498 1779

I felt compelled to register on this site after reading the comments below about my favourite pub in Clapham. If you like a pub that plays an eclectic mix of music, and has polite hardworking bar staff, cosy seating areas, a range of excellent beers (San Miguel, Budvar and Amstel are all on tap), a vast range of non-alcoholic options and a good, and well-priced food menu, then this is the pub for you. Then there's also the lovely decked beer garden, the big conservatory, the excellent pub quiz on Monday nights and a superb weekend brunch (big fry-up, kedgeree, eggs Benedict,

Bloody Marys ...) – I can't say enough good things about this place. Ignore the pretentious rubbish below – or maybe they've only written that to stop more people from coming to this gem of a local?

✎ *Span, November 2005*

A great pub with some mighty fine beers and a great concept with the old workers thing.

✎ *TheGP, August 2004*

Why the (silly) name? The pub takes its name from a song written during a strike of women textile workers in Lawrence, Massachusetts, USA, in 1912.

Twenty-seven thousand women went on strike and marched for 11 weeks to improve their working conditions. Their banners called for bread and roses.

A poet among them, James Oppenheim, wrote these words, which went on to become a famous song for women trade unionists everywhere. The pub is named in recognition of their struggle and the struggle of workers everywhere for a better quality of life for themselves and their families.

✎ *langrabbie, September 2003*

Laidback atmosphere with a good selection of beers on tap, including Leffe and Erdinger.

Great food, especially on a Sunday, when they run an African theme, with food and live music from the featured area.

✎ *jbowman, July 2003*

The Canterbury Arms

Brixton
8 Canterbury Crescent, London SW9 7QD
☎ 020 7274 1711

I recently spent over 12 hours in here over a weekend, so it cannot be that bad! Had to have Boddies most of the time and then on to Guinness when I got bored of that. Excellent atmosphere. Just needs better beers!
✎ *Matthew_of_Ham, December 2005*

Best pub around there that I've found. Great old TV cases. Nice ornate bar. No real ale, but good to hang out in. A dying breed.
✎ *Anonymous, November 2005*

Good pub to meet up in pre-gig. No problem getting served. Not overpriced. Has seating/standing outside.
✎ *snowdog2112, January 2005*

The Cat's Back

Wandsworth
86–88 Point Pleasant, London SW18 1NN

The atmosphere in the pub is great. There was a selection of four real ales on, and the two I sampled were very tasty. Definitely worth going back to.
✎ *salamanda, January 2006*

I was told that that the pub is called The Cat's Back because the owners' cat disappeared once when they were on holiday and they were worried it had gone for good – so a considerate local customer stuck a sign on the pub window 'The Cat's Back' when it reappeared, which the grateful owners saw at once upon returning from holiday.

But yes, Bill, you are right, this is indeed a great pub and it's certainly interesting and different.

P.S. Wonder what the site is worth for its development potential?
✎ JohnBonser, December 2005

Great pub, good beer, interesting and different in a positive way. Only downside is the lack of Mini Cheddars. It's slightly expensive, but worth it. The name of course is a play on the South London joke about the Battersea Dogs Home: 'Do you know the Battersea Dogs Home?' – 'I didn't know he'd been away'.
✎ WandsworthBill, November 2005

Can't really explain what it is that I liked about this place. Could be the excellent range of beers, the interesting collection of (for want of a better word) bric-a-brac, the friendly atmosphere or the log fire. Very different from any other pub I've been to, and all the better for it.
✎ burnsy, November 2005

This is a great little pub full of all sorts of novel knick-knacks and eclectic flotsam and jetsam. Excellent vibe! I can sense, though, that it won't be long before the secret really gets out and the place is invaded by the yuppie brigade with their expensive push-chairs. Enjoy it while you can!
✎ benfuller71, January 2005

An amazing place! This pub well deserves its place in the *Good Beer Guide.* O'Hanlon's beer kept in good condition. An adventurous music policy. Very chilled-out staff make this a refreshing oasis in the Young's heartland. Go there!

✎ *ladnewton, June 2003*

The Clubhouse

Twickenham

✎ 65 Richmond Road, Twickenham, Middlesex TW1 3AW

☎ 020 8404 0095

Agree with other reviewers that this is a very welcome change to the majority of other pubs in and around Twickenham – very friendly, cosy atmosphere. Open fire and games behind the bar were a particular bonus. Good pint of Pride and decent house wine. The food looked good too.

✎ *crusty, January 2006*

Discovered this place shortly after it opened almost three years ago and have spent an unhealthy amount of time there since. A friendlier place you couldn't wish to find, and I have entrusted several important celebratory events to the hospitality of Steve and his staff. They have never failed to impress me, my wife and all my friends with the quality of service, food and drink. Whether it is a quiet early evening drink or a major social occasion, the Clubhouse would always be my first choice.

✎ *AlanW, June 2005*

I adore this pub! Wonderful, warm atmosphere. Very friendly staff who actually take the time to recognise you and greet you warmly.

Amazing food – have tried many places in search of the perfect Sunday roast and I come back here every time. 'Secret' garden in summer is a delight. Haven't experienced the BBQs but a must for this year. A great place to spend a Sunday, either reading the papers or watching the rugby.

Very relaxing. A thoroughly pleasant experience and well recommended.

✎ *Cleversaz, January 2005*

The Cottage

Fulham
21 Colehill Lane, London SW6 5EF
☎ Telephone 020 7736 6217

A real old-fashioned back-street boozer tucked away among the trendy streets of Fulham. The beer is good and the atmosphere is enjoyable, particularly after Fulham FC home games. Well worth a visit if you are tired of the chain pubs that are increasingly dominating the pub landscape.

✎ *gearbox, October 2004*

Made my first visit after Fulham v. Celtic and will be back. Good old-fashioned boozer tucked away in a side street with plenty of space and plenty of staff. It is now running a Sunday-afternoon acoustic session in the back garden, which is enjoyable on a warm afternoon.

✎ *gearbox, July 2004*

The Cricketers

Richmond

The Green, Richmond, Surrey TW9 1LX
☎ 020 8940 4372

Nice pub. Always busy, and yet have often managed to arrive with fortuitous timing and bagged one of the few tables outside. Since these seats are like gold dust in summer, it tends to make you stay longer than you planned, losing yourself and your day people-watching over the green. I discovered the leather sofas on Saturday too – very nice. Excellent service considering the hordes of people needing drinks. Never have to wait very long. They were giving away free iced water in the heatwave a couple of years ago too. Obviously a prime location in the summer, but works well in winter too. A good all-season establishment.
✎ *Cleversaz, July 2005*

A good summer pub. Venture on to the green and watch loads of couples get frisky. Get a room for God's sake! The pub is good though.
✎ *TheGP, July 2005*

Slightly dated interior, but a decent pint and nice location on the green make it worth a visit in the summer when you can sit outside.
✎ *Angus, April 2003*

Right on Richmond Green. Great if you want to get away from the loud pubs that generally inhabit the riverside.
✎ *Mikepcshaw, March 2003*

The Crooked Billet

Wimbledon Common
14 Crooked Billet, London SW19 4RQ
☎ 020 8946 4942

Fantastic. Edgar the 'new' landlord (since the beginning of the year) is an absolute gentleman and doing a great job.

The beer is the best pint of Young's Ordinary to be found in London bar none, and I believe the Special and London Ale have recently won CAMRA awards. Food is good and cheap. Top marks, end of story.
✎ *MrLash, October 2005*

This is a Young's pub. Ate here recently – the food was pretty good and reasonably priced. Good atmosphere and ales too. The serving staff were friendly but were a little too rushed off their feet at times.
✎ *Lopper, April 2005*

Fantastic! Some of the best-kept Young's ales you'll find (and unlike many places, they also know how to keep the lager). Great food – check out the roast-beef baguettes.

Barmaids are delightful, fire is lit in the winter and the seating is comfortable. The only possible downside is that it can get a bit full of smug couples and their offspring at weekends, but they seem to be encouraged towards the large dining room at the back, which is a plus. Great pub!
✎ *MrLash, September 2004*

The Dukes Head

Putney

8 Lower Richmond Road, London SW15 1JN

☎ 020 8788 2552

Reliable Putney boozer that dispenses a fine pint of Special from the main bar (the lounge bar ale can be a little too warm for my taste). Nicely worn-out floor and interior reinforces the fact that many, many people have spent their time wisely here. Sports appear to be shown only in the cramped public bar, leaving plenty of space for the diners to watch the Thames rush by from a comfortable main lounge.

The pub has been graced with the mini-beer festival, from which Burton Beer, a stronger 1960s predecessor to Winter Warmer, is about to be unleashed today for a very limited period. This beer has long been regarded as one of the lost classic ales of London and hasn't been seen on a pump for over 40 years. So what the hell are you waiting for?
✎ *SteveinLondonOctober 2005*

Good no-nonsense original Young's boozer. Warm, comfortable and friendly. Quality of the Ordinary was top-notch. Traditional wooden decor, with big windows overlooking the river. Staff friendly and attracts a decent class of punter. Only criticisms could be that the toilets are a bit scummy, but that's just a detail. One of these is worth a million All Bar Pitcher and Parrots – keep it up!
✎ *MrLash, December 2004*

This should be exhibited on how to keep a pub in its original style, while not letting it get old and rundown. Magnificent big pub,

with traditional fittings and a decent pint. And a Young's pub as well, which makes its success even more surprising.
✎ *TheGP, November 2004*

The Eel Pie

Twickenham
9 Church Street, Twickenham, Middlesex TW1 3NJ
☎ 020 8891 1717

A good real-ale pub. Had four ales and a guest on. Lots of rugby portraits on the wall, and plenty of seating. Pub wasn't too smoky when last I visited. Worth seeking out if you're in the area. In warmer weather there is bench seating on the street outside.
✎ *snowdog2112, February 2005*

A nice pub, with good food and a nice selection of beer. Well ahead of most of the pubs in Twickenham.
✎ *TheGP, August 2004*

One of my favourite pubs. Great Badger Ales in a wonderful location. Always part of our CAMRA group pub crawl when we visit the area.
✎ *JohnnyBGoode, September 2003*

The Effra Hall Tavern

Brixton
38 Kellett Road, London SW2 1EB
☎ 020 7274 4180

Stunning! Good vibe, good beer (at times), cheap and some very cool live music.
✎ *andydsouth, October 2005*

A quality local. Relaxed and friendly with strong customer loyalty.
✎ *redrocket, August 2005*

Best local in Brixton. Good drinks prices – check out the two-pint offers.
✎ *dan_does_pubs, April 2004*

The Jolly Gardners

Putney
61–63 Lacy Road, London SW15 1NT
☎ 020 8780 8921

This is definitely the best pub in Putney. I have spent many a Sunday afternoon at the Jolly, kicking back with a Leffe, playing a board game or two (there is Jenga, Guess Who? and Game Of Life, to name a few – all your kiddie favourites) and listening to some chilled-out Sunday tunes. The food is great and reasonably priced, there is a great range of beers on tap, and it has friendly bar staff and cool clientele. Highly recommended.
✎ *ems, November 2005*

TheClaw is right: this pub is owned by Mitchells & Butlers, as is the Trafalgar on Kings Road. My opinion may be biased as a result of having worked for the manager of this pub a few years back, but he has a knack of turning rubbish boozers into decent pubs with efficient staff (he also did the same with the Hope in

Wandsworth Common, which had been a Firkin), and he has done it again. Having seen what this pub was like before, I'm not sure there can be too many complaints.

✎ *womble54321, September 2005*

Great pub and, I presume, owned and run by the same people that transformed the Trafalgar on the Kings Road? My only gripe is on a Saturday night it gets very busy and some of the bar staff need to keep an eye on those that have been waiting over ten minutes to get served, rather than just serving the pretty girls who wander in. But all in all, a top place for a few beers with mates and have a bite to eat. Long may it continue to remain unspoilt by the Coat and Badge regulars.

✎ *TheClaw, July 2005*

Their Sunday roast is the best I've had in a pub. Relaxed atmosphere – great for whiling away an afternoon reading the papers.

✎ *emily78, February 2004*

The Lord Nelson

Brentford
9 Enfield Road, Brentford, Middlesex TW8 9NY
☎ 020 8568 1877

☆ RAVE REVIEW

This be border country, here. Down in the suburban no-man's land between Ealing and Brentford, recoiling slightly from the booming elevated M4, within sight of the Heathrow flight-path, and becoming cheery mayhem when the Bees are at home, this place has character and homeliness. Diminutive but self-confident landlady Di gave it a makeover a few years ago, so that at least some of the patterned carpet, brown varnish and nicotine were scraped away, surprisingly to reveal a turquoise dado rail and a stripped pine floor. The western extension is Chiswick gastropub, the southern sofa area an Ealing front room, while the east wing retains much of its Aussie/Kiwi robustness, sports screens and at least some residue of an old nautical theme. The only really serious casualty of the turquoise revolution was the western Gents, a godsend to the bibulous and weak-bladdered, who must now orbit the bar in search of relief. Also probably gone are the humorous maritime-themed plates on the loo doors, which said (wait for it, now, folks) 'Buoys' and 'Gulls'. Happy days! The bulldog burgers are worth a special trip, even when you leave the neighbourhood. Di's Sunday lunchtime roast obviates the need for tea or supper. Speaking of dogs, the whole place is benignly ruled over by Bubbles, a minor rhapsody in fluff. Be careful which end you offer peanuts to.

A drawback of Di's relaunch (in addition to the loss of those hilarious loo signs) is that the evening food menu is neither here nor there – we crept out and got a Chinese. The garden is garden-shaped with a fair bit of space, the obligatory decking, plastic children's equipment and a eucalyptus tree whose leaves you can sniff but not pick, thank you very much. Tubes are some way away and Brentford mainline station is not much closer – some kind of E bus reputedly passes nearby. Behave yourself, eat at lunchtime rather than in the evenings, tickle Bubbles' tummy, and you and family can have a good time here. Look out for it from the starboard seats of planes on the final westward approach to LHR, and give us a wave.

✎ *Paul Danon (pauldanon), February 2006*

This pub is terrific. Excellent value on the food front, although I agree about the veggies – could be a bit more adventurous; nevertheless, no real complaints on standard or price. Good selection of wines and very friendly staff and clientele. Has to be the best in Brentford.

✎ *jacinta, February 2006*

Best pub I have come across in this area, which is handy as it happens to be my local. Good selection of beer, with occasional Fuller's guest ales, as well as a good selection of wine and spirits. The food is also excellent – a modern eclectic gastropub-style menu – all home-cooked. However, unlike a gastropub (for example the nearby Ealing Park Tavern), this place has a real atmosphere and is a proper locals' pub.

A bit off the beaten track (hidden away down a back street), but generally this is a good thing – it attracts a loyal and regular crowd of all ages – though it can make its location hard to describe to friends from outside the area. The pub also gets very busy on Brentford match days, although the crowd is always very genial. It is also good for watching sport on TV, with Sky and a big screen. The beer garden is also very nice when we get a nice day (which in Brentford admittedly is not often). All in all, a class act.

✎ *scousemouse, September 2005*

The Magpie and Crown

Brentford
128 High Street, Brentford, Middlesex TW8 8EW
☎ 020 8560 5658

Beer in the Evening

Always an excellent pub. Visited in late 2005. Several friendly people at the bar. Fantastic beer and Thai – not Chinese – food. Recommended. Easy to miss trains from here and get stranded (I haven't, but I know trains from local stations stop early). Check train timetables if using overland – Tubes from Gunnersbury into central London run to about 11.45 p.m.
✎ *ladnewton, January 2006*

Excellent range of beers – very well kept. We went on a Saturday evening and were impressed by the friendly atmosphere there. Bar staff were great and very helpful in calling a taxi at chucking-out time. I will definitely be back.
✎ *NigelW, November 2005*

Interesting place with a Gothic air. Very good beer quality and a variety too. Seems like a really decent local, where effort is made to keep standards high – congratulations!
✎ *mally, July 2005*

This pub is great! The beer is always in fantastic condition and the constantly rotating range is impressive – usually at least one darker beer, which is always appreciated :-) I am by no means a local and can normally only visit maybe once a month, but I have always found the pub friendly and welcoming. I would certainly recommend this establishment to anyone who enjoys drinking proper beer in a proper pub. Cheers!
✎ *Hophead, July 2005*

Great pub and a real oasis for those that like something with a bit more character than chilled fizzy kids' pop to drink. Hundreds of different ales have passed through here – nearly two thousand

since 1996! They're into cask cider too, so if you're looking for a good traditional boozer with great ales, interesting sarnies, a quiz night, etc., you really can't fault this place.
✎ *Prideinside, March 2005*

Molly Malones

Richmond
115–117 Kew Road, Richmond, Surrey TW9 2PN
☎ 020 8940 5486

Much improved since it's under new management: back to the Mollies of old. Nice crowd, decent Guinness, and the new gaffer Anton is a really nice bloke, even if he did play for London Welsh!
✎ *nollag, December 2005*

Great place to watch the rugby. Always pretty busy and with good service.

Used to serve Magners cider before everyone else did. Cheesy bands also play here, which are usually entertaining on a Friday night. Good curry house a couple of doors away as well!
✎ *cathk, April 2005*

I am not a big fan of Guinness, but even I could taste how good a pint it was in here.

Therefore, if you are a fan of the black stuff I would definitely recommend.
✎ *TheGP, March 2005*

The Nightingale

Balham

97 Nightingale Lane, London SW12 8NX

☎ 020 8673 1637

Pretty much all the reviews below are spot on. It's a rare pleasure to come across a proper pub in London and still more surprising to find one run by such friendly people in such an unpretentious manner. Unfortunately for me, the Hope down the road is my nearest pub, but the extra five minutes' walk to here is definitely worth it. Beers are kept well, the food is good, clientele a friendly bunch, and there is a dartboard. Always a recipe for success. Good work!

✎ *womble54321, January 2006*

Just refurbished and, thankfully, Young's have only passed a light hand over this little gem. Not a drop of character has been lost and the improvements to the garden deserve a robust trade in the summer. For some decades, the Nightingale has appealed to all walks of life. It's as if it was the only pub in the village. It certainly does have an almost unique rural charm within London. The management have had the foresight to retain (and build on) that-long standing atmosphere. Almost the last traditional pub in the area. Both beer and food are consistently excellent. Worth travelling to see it.

✎ *ianbeer, November 2005*

Having used this pub regularly for some time, I endorse the other comments. It is a very welcoming local and sometimes gets busy due to its popularity.

The clientele is varied and the staff friendly. My hat off to Joannie and management (new) for keeping the pub traditional.
✎ *keredn, March 2005*

Superb! The new management are dedicated to keeping this as a traditional pub. That's very rare in this area. Thorough refurbishment due in April 2005 but as a pub and not a bar/concept etc., etc. Will remain very strong on support for local charities. A remarkable house. Totally welcoming to all and fast becoming unique. Well done the new hosts – who know me only by sight, so no bias in this comment.
✎ *ianbeer, March 2005*

The Park Tavern

Southfields
212 Merton Road, London SW18 5SW
☎ 020 8488 8855

My new local. Nice atmosphere, decent pint of 6X, friendly bar staff, courtyard garden. Large sofas at the front of the bar, and more seating at the side. No TV, which (strangely) I found to be a blessing. New owners have done a good job on the refurb – smartening the place up while ensuring it still looks like a pub.

My only complaints would be that there are not enough seats, and that the area with tables in the saloon bar is very open and a bit barn-like. Otherwise, good job. I'll be back this weekend to sample the food. And the beer.
✎ *burnsy, October 2005*

Always looked like a bit of a old man's pub so I'd never bothered going in there before the refurb. Went in for a few last night and was very impressed. Service from the (very friendly) landlord was great and the 6X was on great form – unusual for London. Massive comfy sofas and a decent-looking menu with reasonably priced food. I look forward to commandeering sofas for long winter days of beery fun. I really hope this place does well. It'll be good competition for the Earl Spencer.

✎ *MrLash, September 2005*

As noted by others, the eagerly awaited refurb has been completed and doesn't disappoint. The courtyard garden is a big plus and will be great for the summer. The menu looks good (made me eager to stay and eat despite other plans last night) and the mix of tables and comfy seating seem really well balanced. Had a good pint of draught San Miguel. Will be back to check on the ales soon ...

✎ *OJ360, June 2005*

The Priory Arms

Stockwell

83 Lansdowne Way, London SW8 2PB

☎ 020 7622 1884

This pub may not have a prime location, situated as it is on a back street among the Stockwell housing estates, but it is a real gem. The major selling point may be the beer, superb in both range and quality, but the food is also excellent. The Sunday lunches are unusually good for a pub roast. The wine list is also extensive, including many fruit wines. If you live in the Stockwell or Vauxhall area and like your real ales, then you won't do better than the Priory Arms. In fact, I only wish there were a couple of other pubs in the area that sold beer half as good.

✎ *Chris F, September 2005*

A gem. Lovely atmosphere and great for leisurely roast and Sunday papers.

✎ *redrocket, August 2005*

Lovely pub, although a bit pricey. Worth a visit for a great selection of fruit beers, and food quite good too. Close to nearby Lambeth College, but luckily too expensive for most of the students, so it maintains a relaxed, local atmosphere.

✎ *vinrouge, May 2005*

Gary and Nickie have retired and passed the pub on to a new licensee. He promises to keep the pub exactly as it is – that is, a vibrant local freehouse with an excellent range of real ales, together with a top-class bottled-lager selection. After I visited with a group of friends on a Friday, I was reassured that the pub remains in good hands for the foreseeable future. And, sad though it is to miss Gary and Nickie, the news that the pub is safe can only be welcomed in these circumstances.

✎ *ladnewton, December 2004*

A really good pub, a wide range of beer and plenty of room to relax. No piped music either.

✎ *beeronaut, July 2004*

This is among London's best pubs. The very friendly, informed, chilled-out and enthusiastic management rubs off on the enjoyment of all customers. Harveys seems to be a regular beer, plus there is a constantly changing range of up to four other guests. I was there on a Friday with four friends and we were introduced to an exquisite German beer – a subject on which the landlord is well-informed and well-travelled. An impressive stock is held, and some people come just for the German beers. Even the dog (I'm no dog lover) is friendly. I would recommend this pub to anyone looking for a great pint in a great atmosphere. No music, allowing for great conversation. A gem!

✎ *ladnewton, April 2003*

The Railway Tavern

Hampton Wick

91 High Street, Hampton Wick, Kingston upon Thames, Surrey KT1 4DG

☎ 020 8614 1111

☆ RAVE REVIEW

The Railway is a legend in its own drinking-up time. Standing at one end of a small but well-pubbed village between Teddington and Kingston, it welcomes everyone, from its regulars to students from the local universities, to thirsty commuters from the station opposite. With all of the features that one would expect from a traditional pub, it has a lot more beside, possessing character in spades.

Thought to be the oldest building in the village and a former coaching inn, it has colourful history of its own, not least of which involves some of its former landlords. My good friend Mick Jordan was the guv'nor when my wife Colette and I first chanced across it on the night the Republic of Ireland beat Italy in the 1994 World Cup. Mick paid little heed to the licensing laws and many a great night was had as a result.

Mick called it a day in 1998 and next behind the wheel was charismatic American John Stryker. John improved the decor and developed the food side and the fun continued much as it had, until one fateful day in late 2003, when his past as an FBI fugitive caught up with him.

Since then it's been in the capable hands of Rachel Brisland, who arrived to take the tiller at the height of the Stryker intrigue – and not a moment too soon.

Now food-free, it can be a quieter place during the week, but many regular faces hit the place on a Friday night. Live music has always been a feature of the Railway. With a pleasant beer garden, a jukebox, pool table, darts and TVs showing live sport, you'd be hard pressed to find a better traditional boozer in an area that's seen many sold for redevelopment. Visit it soon!

✎ *Al Ferrier, February 2006*

The Red Lion

Isleworth
92–94 Linkfield Road, Isleworth, Middlesex TW7 6QJ
☎ Telephone 020 8560 1457

Finally got myself over here a few weeks ago – what a lovely boozer! Excellent beer range, wide range of events, gigs, etc., and pleasant garden out back. Only slight irritation: the regulars tend to occupy a line of stools along the bar so you have to order your ale from behind or between them. But I can live with that.

✎ *E17Bee, September 2005*

Quite like the pub – interior could do with a bit of a spruce-up, but nice garden. (Same carpet for the past 50 years I think.) Definitely an interesting selection of beers, but whoever is in charge of selecting them has a definite and unwelcome bias for light-coloured summer ales – in fact, nearly every beer they sell is of this type. A few more traditional best bitters with at least a quarter-inch of head on them and a nice brown colour wouldn't go amiss. (And I'm not even from Oop North.)

✎ *Jethro2, August 2005*

Remarkable rare example of a real pub and well deserving its status as one of the 12 best CAMRA-rated pubs in Greater London. Amazing selection of perfectly kept real ales, with nine guest ales changing daily. Separate public bar for the sports watchers, the pool players and jukebox listeners. Live blues music on Saturdays and Sundays. Traditional Sunday lunches. Two great beer festivals every year, with over 50 real ales! Wish I lived nearer, but it is only two minutes from the railway station.

✎ *Flyonthewall, November 2004*

This is not a half-bad pub. Good ales, beer garden and music.

✎ *TheGP, August 2004*

I really enjoy the live music and the excellent range of quality real ales. There is a bar for each facility and a good outdoor area for the beer festivals and theatrics/charity events.

✎ *JohnnyBGoode, September 2003*

The Roebuck

Richmond Hill
130 Richmond Hill, Richmond, Surrey TW10 6RN
☎ 020 8948 2329

I love this pub to pieces. It was my regular while I worked nearby. It is close to the American University nearby, but used only by the staff – not the students. Beer is very nice and the 'new' food menu is all one can expect from a pub, plus a bit more. Interesting bar staff and regulars. The separate rooms have their own personalities and their own familiar faces. Drinkers are able to take their glasses over the road on to the famous view and watch the sunset over the river if they wish.
✎ *Rayzer, January 2006*

Best pub in London, bar none, Marie and Paul have been running it for nearly seven years now. All the staff give a warm welcome, food is reasonably priced and beer is well kept. Great pub for meeting up with friends or warming up in after a jaunt round Richmond Park.
✎ *Bezmina, December 2005*

Good beer, good atmosphere. True – not much in the way of music and no television for sports. Must be the type of place where you bring friends and actually talk.
✎ *Mr.Matt, May 2005*

Incredible view, great grub, Trivial Pursuit, and you're utterly removed from the teeming cess pit that is Richmond High Street. Go there!
✎ *loads_of_monkeys, April 2004*

The Rose and Crown

Clapham Old Town

2 The Polygon, London SW4 0JG

☎ 020 7720 8265

Very unpretentious for the area. Great frontage (the building – the barmaid was nice too, though, and helpful).

Ale in good nick. Would pop in for another.
✎ *mitomighty, November 2005*

Proper old pub. Staff efficient and friendly without being annoying. Beer well kept. Best place in Clapham to spend some time with some good beer.
✎ *jorrocks, October 2005*

It doesn't get much better than this. Only spoilt by the public-school hooray henries who ruined the England v. Croatia victory by talking inanely about property, rugger and all the other little foibles of the fecklessly rich and stupid during the game.

And not celebrating properly when we won it.

Stick to the wine bars, Jeremy and Rupert.
✎ *conniwot, June 2005*

Good beer and very friendly. When my food took all of 15 minutes to arrive, I was given a free half!
✎ *drtimthornton, November 2003*

The Rose and Crown

Tooting Bec
140 Tooting Bec Road, London SW17 8BH
☎ 020 8672 2691

What I like about this place is that everyone wants to have a good time here and if you avoid London football games everyone is really nice and a mixed bunch and they seem to want you to have a good time too. The staff are removed but spot on.

The landlord seems to know the coup. I love footie but would generally avoid watching it here, but if I had a spare evening at the weekend I would come here every Saturday night.
✎ *Anonymous, December 2005*

My local. Not the brightest of pubs, but clean, safe and fun. On the plus side: good clean beer, big screen for football, nice management/bar staff, good mix of people (usually) and hilarious karaoke complete with Elvis. On the down side: Chelsea fans aplenty, beer isn't cheap and they don't do any munchies. Overall: 8/10.
✎ *Dr. T, December 2005*

The bar with the footie is a bit Boycey but OK, but the real delight is the karaoke evenings at the weekend. Marvellous!

You'll be surprised at what you see – professional-level yodelling, spoon-playing, opera singers, the obligatory Elvis. Great stuff! A decent local.
✎ *mitomighty, November 2005*

The Spirit Bar Cafe

Tooting

94 Tooting High Street, London SW17 0RR
☎ 020 8767 3311

Probably about the best place to drink at the Broadway end of Tooting. Friendly staff and a good spot to watch the football.
✎ *primalpete, November 2005*

Just returned to the area again and got a great surprise when I revisited Spirit. Music is still really good and food has improved from the stuff they used to do. I tried their homemade Thai chicken burger on one night and the Sunday roast with friends last week.

It rocks! Good value and great quality for Tooting. Staff seemed really friendly and made me feel like I'd been a regular for years. Decor has improved but needs updating, although it has a good relaxed feel about it. Will definitely be visiting here more often. My only wish is that they make it non-smoking.
✎ *Anonymous, September 2005*

Even though this place is tiny, it's a real gem. Friendly staff and good beers and spirits on offer, plus plenty of seating. Not much standing room, and can get very hot and smoky at night.

Plenty of room to chill out back, and good views of plasma screens for the sport. My only complaint is that they'd turn the ruddy music down in the back room so you don't have to shout to communicate.
✎ *Flawed, September 2005*

The Spread Eagle

Wandsworth

71 Wandsworth High Street, London SW18 2PT
☎ 020 8877 9809

Went in there again and JohnBonser's comment about it not being a youngsters' pub was an understatement times two. I didn't see anyone under 50! However, the ale was absolutely spot on as it should be, being so close to the brewery. And almost a full selection of Young's bottled beers.

The pub inside and out is fantastic-looking, and the open fires were going. OK, it is full of old gits, but they've got character and there has always been plenty of extra space. Give it a try – it's not a place for a crazy night on the pull, but it is a place for 'one of those nights'. 10/10 for decor and beers, 9/10 for charismatic old fellas, 7/10 for service, and 4/10 for excitement outside of the aforementioned categories. All food £3.99 between 12 and 3 p.m. and then 6 and 9 p.m. Anyone know how good/bad it is?
✎ *Anonymous, December 2005*

Fine traditional Young's pub. Worth visiting just to admire the spledid glasswork. Not a youngsters' pub, and all the better for it.
✎ *JohnBonser, March 2005*

A great, traditional Young's pub.

Nice friendly staff, good beer (tried the Ordinary) and very tasty paninis are served most of the day. Definitely worth a visit.
✎ *ladnewton, November 2003*

The St. Margaret's Tavern

St Margaret's

107 St Margarets Road, Twickenham, Middlesex TW1 2LJ

☎ 020 8892 2369

Still love it! Would be absolutely fantastic if you could get some more tables and chairs outside though. It's a shame you can't use some of that carpark.

✎ *pinot, June 2005*

I don't know what it was like before the refit but, whatever they did, they did it right. I'm particularly impressed at its self-declared 'football-free zone'. This pub is busy no matter when you go in. Getting served is never a problem at the bar, no matter how packed it is, although table service can be a bit slow – I've also had to go to the bar and ask on several occasions. Great for spotting rugby players and the odd person you recognise off the telly. Excellent quiz on a Tuesday. Extensive menu so you're always spoilt for choice. Friendly bar staff. Food turns up pretty promptly and is delicious – swaddled beef indeed! I'd also recommend salmon linguine – in fact I may have to go there this afternoon ... Definitely worth many visits.

✎ *Cleversaz, May 2005*

This is a great pub with lovely food and a good selection of real ales, along with decent wines, bottles of world beers and the very tasty Kronenbourg Blanc. Bar service has always been good whenever I've been, and the food service is top notch too (although I would agree that it's annoying to go to the bar to order something, only to be told you have to go and sit back down and

wait while they send someone over). Quiz night is to be recommended and the live music is good too (although perhaps a little loud if you're too close). Definitely worth a visit.
✎ *wavey, May 2004*

The Sultan

South Wimbledon
78 Norman Road, London SW19 1BN
☎ 020 8542 4532

Superbly kept good-value Hop Back ales. Bar staff friendly, and Dillon the dog and Migsy the cat make for a great atmosphere. Lighting and table arrangement could do with improvement.

BBQs in summer.
✎ *FrankDS, May 2005*

Mmmm ... the Entire, GFB and Summer/Winter Lightning (from the Hop Back Brewery) are well worth a look, as is the bottled Crop Circle from the same place. Very nice!
✎ *Alexh1982, December 2003*

This pub should be kept secret from the rest of the world – it's that good! Good beers, great atmosphere, traditional pub.
✎ *Pompeybob, October 2003*

A very pleasant, unpretentious and quiet pub. Excellent, well-kept beers: Summer Lightning, GFB, etc.
✎ *howardhopkins, September 2003*

Great back-street local. I managed to visit it on its opening night several years ago. Owned by Hop Back Brewery from Wiltshire – try the GFB and, even better, the Summer Lightning.
✎ *Simonf, June 2003*

The Surprise

Stockwell
16 Southville, London SW8 2PP
☎ 020 7622 4623

Very nice, quiet, old-fashioned back-street pub. No music playing – just the clink of glasses and pleasant sounds of human conversation.
✎ *beermann, December 2005*

Small but just about perfectly formed. A countryside feel in the heart of darkest south London.
✎ *redrocket, August 2005*

It took me by surprise. Great small pub with Young's beer and dog. What more could one want?
✎ *Anonymous, May 2005*

Outdoor seating by the park is as pleasant as it gets in Stockwell, although the pub is quite small and smoky inside.

Friendly staff and well-priced beer, but the dog has to go on a diet – it can hardly walk!
✎ *vinrouge, May 2005*

The Tide End Cottage

Teddington
8 Ferry Road, Teddington, Middlesex TW11 9NN
☎ 020 8977 7762

Just a brilliant pub! Went in there on Sunday for a roast as have recently bought a puppy and heard it was dog-friendly, and it was great! They have dog treats behind the bar and all the staff were really friendly. And the food was great.
✎ *stones, November 2005*

Been using the Tide End regularly for many years. Still one of the friendliest and most authentic pubs in Teddington.

Reasonably priced (by today's standards), well-kept beer, pleasant staff, and not ruined by a brewery's vision of what a modern pub should be.
✎ *gordonw, September 2005*

First-class pub. Possibly the best in Teddington.
✎ *TheGP, May 2005*

The Town Wharf

Old Isleworth
Swan Street, Isleworth, Middlesex TW7 6RJ
☎ 020 8847 2287

Always loved this pub, Went there last night with friend, and she really loved it. You have to go to pubs further along the Thames to get this close to the river, either up- or down-stream, but none of them is as comfortable or as welcoming.

✎ *zagreb, October 2005*

I like this pub. The food is really nice and it's an ideal place to go as a couple for a few quiet drinks. Wednesdays are usually livelier though, as they have the pub quiz, which is quite good fun.

✎ *kerrya, March 2005*

Magnificent pub. Its only fault, which is a major one, is it's a real ass to get to. Sam Smith's pubs are always the bee's knees for best beers and prices, so you can't go wrong really, as long as you can get home easily.

✎ *TheGP, August 2004*

The Trafalgar Arms

Tooting
148 Tooting High Street, London SW17 0RT
☎ 020 8767 6059

Quite a decent pub. Can be pretty quiet when the med students are not around. Good space out front to sit in the summer, even if it is right by the main road. Pretty odd mix of drinkers, but friendly enough.

✎ *primalpete, November 2005*

Lived opposite for three years, so has a place in me heart. Hopefully still run by Trevor (a bear of a man with a lurid Mohican). Candlelit ambience attracts a good cross-section, from gay couples

to raucous nurses from nearby St George's. Good to sit outside on a hot day. The roast dinners are fabulous.
✎ *beeker, June 2004*

Good evenings to be had here. Can be vibrant and cosy at the same time. Everything lit by candlelight.

Speedy staff. Only downside it can get really smoky in there.
✎ *Flawed, February 2004*

The Trinity Arms

Brixton
45 Trinity Gardens, London SW9 8DR
☎ 020 7274 4544

Brilliant. The beers (the usual Young's range) are always in top condition. Though Young's bitter is not my favourite, it's always a pleasure in the Trinity. The pub has a good, relaxed feel, and as it's not visible from the high street it doesn't get too rammed.

It's not too loud and I've never been unable to find a seat, so it's the perfect meeting place before heading off to the beer hell that they call the Brixton Academy.
✎ *red, December 2005*

Great pub that has waylaid me on pretty much every food shopping trip I've ever tried to make in Brixton.
✎ *Beermeup, September 2005*

If you live around Brixton and the family is visiting, this is the place to take Granny. Nice, clean, friendly pub. Treasured by locals and those not up for 'vibrant' Brixton.

✎ *redrocket, August 2005*

Good Young's pub (i.e. good beer and rubbish wallpaper) hidden down a street in Brixton. If you're in the area and you don't fancy getting crushed and deafened in a trendy place or sitting like a pleb in a Wetherspoon's or Goose, then go here. The vibe was quite gentle when I was there, and this is certainly where the richer end of Brixtonians come.

✎ *MrScott, December 2004*

The White Cross

Richmond

Water Lane, Richmond, Surrey TW9 1TJ

☎ 020 8940 6844

Sorted! Where else can you enjoy a nice pint or two of Young's while watching the incoming tide cover the stupidly parked cars? A real gem.

✎ *Matthew_of_Ham, December 2005*

A price of Young's Bitter is £2.45 – great value for what is a lovely pub with a great view of the river and the world passing by. Lager is more expensive so don't drink it, because it ain't worth it. A great pub on a sunny afternoon but avoid at weekends when the riverside at Richmond is clogged with people.

✎ *gearbox, June 2005*

Young's Special well kept. Lively crowd of the Richmond gentry. Great location along the Thames, with outdoor seating in the garden and on the balcony. Lovely view from the windows. Walking distance from transportation. Bar staff quick to serve. All in a pub that actually has been around a while. What more can you look for?
✎ *Mr.Matt, May 2005*

A perfect place to start the weekend on a Friday night watching the world (and some very attractive women) pass by as you sup a pint of Young's. Stella at £3.20 is about the most expensive I have encountered, but it is worth it for the location and the atmosphere of the place.
✎ *gearbox, July 2004*

Great pub with a very friendly atmosphere and well worth including in any pub crawl of Richmond.
✎ *Angus, March 2003*

The White Horse

Parsons Green
1–3 Parson's Green, London SW6 4UL
☎ 020 7736 2115

Met a friend who's back in the country for a couple of weeks here last night. I've been before and was aware of the Sloaney leanings, but if you want excellent beer and food served by knowledgeable and attentive staff then it's definitely worth learning to live with the other clientele. Or alternatively, fill it with enough like-minded people so that they have to go to Aragon House.
✎ *OJ360, February 2006*

Beer in the Evening

Had been looking forward to visit this beer and food Mecca for years, and last September I had the opportunity to pay a visit. Nice range of beers on cask in the bar. After moving into the dining area on the ground floor, we were presented with an impressive food menu, with beer recommendations. Exquisite food and beer! As a dessert, we had Fuller's Vintage Ale 2002 and Harvey Imperial Extra Double Stout.
✎ *Finn, October 2005*

A premier-league pub in London. An enormous range of international bottled beers and well-kept real ales should tempt even the least inquisitive of identikit lager drinkers. Whether dining in the courtyard restaurant or supping outside in the front garden overlooking the green, attacking the seemingly year-round burgers on the BBQ, this place is difficult to beat. Exceptionally good are the seasonal real ale weekend festivals, which seem to attract people from the far reaches of the capital, all enjoying the splendid selection of unusual beers (many never usually found inside the M25). Coming here can be an addiction that is very hard to shake off.
✎ *SteveinLondonDecember 2004*

Have only visited on warm sunny lunchtimes when there was a choice of seats outside opposite the green or in the comparatively empty interior, with its comfy sofas. Good selection of real ales and quality (but pricey) lunches. Ploughman's particularly good.
✎ *lout_from_the_lane, May 2004*

Fantastic pub! The food is excellent but a bit pricey. The range of Belgian beers is great, including the delicious Chimay on draught. Is known as the 'Sloaney Pony', due to its clientele!
✎ *Angus, May 2003*

The White Swan

Richmond
Old Palace Lane, Richmond, Surrey TW9 1PG
☎ 020 8940 0959

Fantastic food. If you want to eat here on a weekend, book well in advance. A really nice place for a drink too.
✎ *pinot, December 2005*

Friendly pub serving several well-kept real ales, including London Pride and Bombardier.
✎ *alewhale, November 2005*

This is a truly first-rate pub. Out of the way of the rest of Richmond, so you get none of the Hounslow chavs ruining the atmosphere.

A very nice pub for a civilised drink.
✎ *TheGP, July 2005*

Secluded and comfortable pub that does good Sunday lunches, but get there before 2 p.m. or they may have run out of food.

That's how popular it is – but not a reflection on the catering abilities as such!
✎ *beeronaut, May 2005*

Lovely little place. Tucked away, so you won't find it unless you know where to look. Great garden in summer.
✎ *Cleversaz, January 2005*

The White Swan

Twickenham
Riverside, Twickenham, Middlesex TW1 3DN
☎ 020 8892 2166

The dog pub! There were more dogs than people in here last time I was in, but a quality place – lovely atmosphere, friendly staff, real fire in winter, loads of outside seating and BBQ in summer. Great when it gets cut off by the floods: 'Oh no! We'll have to buy another pint!'
✎ *Cleversaz, January 2005*

This is a charming, if outrageously expensive, pub. Definitely in a lovely location though, and in the summer especially.
✎ *TheGP, August 2004*

Tucked away down a side street, which makes it difficult to find, but that is part of the charm. I was there on Saturday and the pub was virtually empty – everybody was out in the beer garden across the road, which is right alongside the river. Great atmosphere and well worth a visit. One of the best boozers in the area. However, I do feel that something could be done to improve the quality of the toilets, which are distinctly nineteenth century.
✎ *gearbox, July 2004*

The Willoughby Arms

Kingston upon Thames
Willoughby Road, Kingston upon Thames, Surrey KT2 6LN
☎ 020 8546 4236

Again, flawless – went to the Halloween Beer Fest on Saturday. No other reason to visit Kingston really. Great beer, great people, good music and sport on the telly. Will attempt to get to one of the Ale Wednesdays. This pub is a gem.

✎ *darloexile, October 2005*

A brilliant back-street pub that has everything going for it.

This really is an example of how good pubs can be with the right landlord and staff. It puts many of Kingston's other pubs (particularly the managed outlets alongside the river) to shame in terms of the quality of the experience.

✎ *gearbox, June 2005*

Excellently run pub. Rick does a fantastic job, and has even managed to get this lager man drinking real beer. Food is basic pub grub, but is cheap and good quality. BBQ on summer weekends are great. Pool table is nice and the sport's nearly always on, despite there being a football-over-rugby bias.

✎ *I_Love_Rugby, June 2005*

Excellent pub, lively, friendly, a wide range of a guest ales and a fiendish quiz on Sunday nights.

✎ *barnstormer, February 2005*

Woodies

New Malden
Thetford Road, New Malden, Surrey KT3 5DY
☎ 020 8949 5824

Beer in the Evening

I hadn't been there for a few years until last night. Glad to say it was just as good as I remember it. Great beer and a remarkable, unique interior.
✎ *DeviousDave, November 2005*

Seven real ales, four regular and three guests – apart from other top-pressure and lagers, ciders, etc. Now that is a proper pub!
✎ *Anonymous, October 2005*

Still the best pub in New Malden by a country mile, but these are worrying times. The new landlady is very nice, but the new quiz is rubbish compared with the old, Pete-based one, and this makes me very sad. Nothing ever lasts forever, I suppose.
✎ *newmalden, February 2004*

Good, good beer. An out-of-the-way gem.
✎ *DeviousDave, January 2003*

The Wych Elm

Kingston upon Thames
93 Elm Road, Kingston upon Thames, Surrey KT2 6HT
☎ 020 8546 3271

We have been to this pub twice for jazz evenings – both very enjoyable. Manny and Margaret are great hosts, and the locals are very friendly. A range of Fuller's real ales are on tap and the white wine was enjoyed by my wife. For an outsider, the Kingston one-way systems and parking problems must be overcome, but it is worth it in the end.
✎ *pburton, January 2006*

Wonderful – a real traditional pub, but clean and fantastically friendly. The bar staff are lovely. Just don't tell too many people!
✎ *patsy, January 2006*

A great local, serving quality real ale and with comfortable seating and a good atmosphere. Not too smoky. Good service. One of the best in this area. It has won CAMRA awards.
✎ *Fab4Rovers, November 2005*

Superb! In an area that is keen to pursue yuppiedom to the max, the WE is really doing the business. Close to several other decent pubs – try a crawl! Manny sells the best Pride in the whole of Kingston. It's an unusual shape too, featuring a traditional public bar and a larger, more open-plan saloon. There's a large garden too. They have regular barbeques and feature live jazz sometimes, but I can forgive them for that. A very comfortable and quite friendly pub. Come for the ale and stay for the welcome. Cheers!
✎ *NewMaldenOrder, August 2005*

Thanks

We'd like to thank all the people who have left comments and reviews on the website over the years. In particular, the people whose words have been used in this book:

154e, 3DoorsDown, abacus3, ahscum, AlanW, Albert_Campion, Ale_Bloke, alewhale, alexdelarge, Alexh1982, almost_an_old_git, Amanda_Fuller, amleyland, amphalon, andrew1961, andydsouth, Angus, AnotherYankeePoof13, AshingdonMan, baggyjim, barnetblackdog, barnstormer, beeker, beerbaby, beerbum63, Beerbunter, beermann, Beermeup, beeronaut, benfuller71, Bewitched, Bezmina, bigaerials, bigbeerbelly, BigPete, billiliu, billy124, Billy_and_Me, BinBagBob, Boaby, bonsai, Boothers, Boss_Hog, bossygirl, Bovine_Juice, brasco, brionyot, brodie_bruce, bron1allen, bub, bumpby, burnsy, BusterGut, cackgsy, cafc, canastajim, cannon1882, cardamom, carterse9, casual66, cathk, Chantil, Chelsea_Loyal, chipawayboy, chippysupper, ChrisF, chrisgill33, cid, cider_murray, CJB, Claret_and_blue, Cleversaz, conniwot, crimsonpirate, crusty, Curly_Helen, D.Bookless, dan...rodney, dan_does_pubs, danny_cascarino, danrkelly, darloexile, Darren_in_the_City, dave-boden, Davepearce, DaveTheDog, davetherave, davidb, dawnage, deptford_joe, DeviousDave, dgriffin, DJ.Alexander, DKavanagh, Dr.T, Dr_Cirrohsis, Dr_J, drbee, DrewSavage, drtimthornton, duncan, dwaine, Dylarolla, E17Bee, E1_Norton, elllie, elmothelime, emily78, Emmett, ems, eric1, Fab4Rovers, fatshirt, FattusBlokus, Finn, FISHTHEMOD, flat3, Flawed, Flyonthewall,

Beer in the Evening

FrankDS, fromedrinker, full_english, ganger, Gann, gatecrasher, gearbox, georgebridges, Gerontay, Get_me_some_Old_Tom, Gibboski, gilesd, gingerweasel, gizmo, gjs34, gordonw, graley, grapat, Graylob, gryn, gussetmonkey, Hal, harlequin, hazey, Hockers, hooley, HOPEDIXON, Hophead, Hoppo, howardhopkins, I_Love_Rugby, ianbeer, intermelocal, jacinta, jackthelad, JamesDaff, jaq, jaykoivu, JazHaz, jbowman, jcraf, jedibond, Jesper, Jet, jethro, Jethro2, jhawkins, jhsp, Joe_Cundy, joeadams, JohnBonser, JohnMcC, JohnnyBGoode, JohnWallace, jollid, JollyGreenGiant, jorrocks, jossv, Juancoffee, kabyar, katya_1978, keep_it_green, keredn, kerrya, kmcs, kodabar, krylon76, ladnewton, landormick, langrabbie, Lawrence_M, leggless, Lembo, lennie384, libero, Linkman, lipster, lizziewill, loads_of_monkeys, Loki, longfella, Lopper, Lord_bangstick, lordhicks, lout_from_the_lane, LovePubs, lozatron, lubyloo, lucy_k, lynshroom, M.Sticker, M_Evans, Madcap, maddiekat, mally, MarcDickson, MarkW, martineaux, Martinl, marty21, marty_mac, Matthew_of_Ham, mattmbaker, mattyd, McDrunk, Medicrob1, Mike_McCabe, mikecharles_mjc, mikem, Mikepcshaw, MikeyBee, mikez, Millay, MissKitty, misterpercy, misty_night, mitomighty, mmmpktge, moncrief, Moose58, Mr.Matt, Mr.Monkfish, Mr.Raffles, mr_lunch, mrfalafel, mrfrisky, MrLash, MrScott, mrsjones, MrSOBA, Muffindamule, Muzthing, mym, Nailed, newmalden, NewMaldenOrder, nick.t, nido, NigelW, nollag, nonstick, oak_cliff, oakleym, OCW, OJ360, OldRogue, oxenhill-shaw, pablos13, Paintbrush, palser, Pat72, patrickjsm, patsy, pauldanon, Paulie, paulmartin, pburton, persist_artist, Pertwee, peshwengi, peterthebeetle, pgazz, PieFace, pinot, pint_o_mild_please, PMH273, Pompeybob, pompeylass, Prideinside, primalpete, pub_numpty, pubcollector, PunkySi, Quinno, Rah_24, Raimundo, Rayzer, Real_Al, rebelde, red, redrocket, Regis, Rich66, rl3_hill, robbie2005, robinson, rockstar, RogerB, ronnierosenthal, roryog, Ruby, rubywillow, rune, s2thafizzle, saiga, salamanda, scareyd, scousemouse, Shelders, SILVERARROW, silverside, simon_barman, Simonf, skorch, slb, Slipperduke, Sm1, smiley, snowdog2112, southdown12jack, spacekadet, Span, SSSS, SteveinLondonStonch, stoner, stones, stringerdax, stripe, stuartwigby, SusanC, sussexsketch, tanderson7, Terry_W, tgould, tharg, the_sarah_day_fan_club, thebigman, TheClaw, TheGP, TheHorsesMouth, TheIrishC, tim_eyles, TimJones, timkholman, Tiny, Tiser, TJR, TomAngel, TonyAle, tonyandrachel, tonymontana, tour_contact, tpk1, Trapdoor, triphere, Tuna, Ullage, vic_of_india, Vindaloo, vinrouge, W980501, WandsworthBill, wavey, Wayne_Jordan, wilbur101, Wild_John, Will2, winkywoo, Winstonunderwood, wmon, womble54321, Woolyback, wpjh, writtleman, yamin, yoooreds, young_camra_collectiv, yourhardkorehero, zagreb, zakman, Zaphod

Special thanks go to the people who wrote reviews just for this book:

Al Ferrier, Andrew Lipscombe (lipster), Paul Danon (pauldanon), Phil Wilson, Scott Allin (Mr.Monkfish), Simon, Stephen Batty (stephen.batty)

Indexes

Find pubs by feature

Find pubs by place

Beer in the Evening

Beer in the Evening

Find pubs by name

Beer in the Evening